ON BEING
WOUNDED

ON BEING
WOUNDED

EDWARD W WOOD JR

Fulcrum Publishing
Golden, Colorado

Book design by Hugh Anderson, Archetype, Inc.
Cover photograph, Poster Walk for Disarmament, courtesy of Fellowship of
Reconciliation

The author would like to thank the following for their permission to reprint:

Excerpt from "Burnt Norton" in *Four Quartets*, copyright 1943 by T. S. Eliot
and renewed 1971 by Esme Valerie Eliot, reprinted by permission of Harcourt Brace
Jovanovich, Inc., and Faber and Faber Limited.

Excerpt from *The Poems of Gerard Manley Hopkins*, Fourth Edition, edited
by W. H. Gardner and N. H. MacKenzie, courtesy of Oxford University Press.

Excerpt from "Song-Books of the War" from *Collected Poems* by Siegfried
Sassoon. Copyright 1918, 1920 by E. P. Dutton. Copyright 1936, 1946, 1947, 1948
by Siegfried Sassoon. Used by permission of Viking Penguin, a division of Penguin
Books USA Inc. World rights by permission of George Sassoon.

Library of Congress Cataloging-in-Publication Data

Wood, Edward W., Jr.
    On being wounded / Edward W. Wood, Jr.
        p.   cm.
    ISBN 1-55591-076-9
    1. Wood, Edward W., Jr. 2. Veterans—United States—Biography. 3. Mascu-
linity (Psychology) 4. Violence—United States—Psychological aspects. 5. World
War, 1939–1945—Veterans—United States. I. Title.
U53.W628A3 1991
362.86'092—dc20
[B]   91–71368
                                                                             CIP

Printed in the United States of America

0 9 8 7 6 5 4 3 2 1

Fulcrum Publishing
350 Indiana Street
Golden, Colorado 80401

CONTENTS

This book is dedicated to all young men in their teens and twenties killed or wounded in any war, and to the members of the Seventh Armored Division and the French Resistance,

and

to members of my family who endured the consequences of

my wound:

my mother

my father

Alma

and my children

PREFACE

I journeyed into the land of the wounded, into its strange dimensions and despairs, from a time and a place when war was glorified, the proper sphere of manhood. My father and his male ancestors served in every war in which my nation had fought since its founding. My great-great-uncle was wounded in the Civil War at Cold Harbor, fighting for the Union; my great-grandfather served in the Confederate Army and was wounded at Munfordville. The blood memory of the rifles of my fathers merged into the mellifluous voices of my many mothers—the heritage which led me, voluntarily, to war.

As a boy of nineteen, I was badly wounded in the liberation of France on September 7, 1944. That wound, that time of combat, irrevocably changed my life. This book is about those changes, the explosion of my personal universe. It is written in this century of technological warfare for all those, soldier or civilian, injured in firefight or rebellion; for those of my generation who, near the end of life, search for the meaning of their years of war; for those of middle age who struggle with career and marriage and family, sometimes still lost in the terrible memories of their youth; for those of adolescence, meat for the butcher, trapped in the barbarity of war in third-world nations.

My account chronicles the process of loss, repression, rediscovery, acceptance, and it describes the terrible rage and bitterness which often follow a wounding, as well as their gradual, painful resolution.

In this century of war little has been reported from the land of the wounded, though it exists within all nations and among all generations. This book narrates my lifelong journey through this land, its terrors and triumphs, its landscape and its boundaries, its despairs and delights—and, most of all, the special quality my wounding has given to my search for compassion in this century of war.

WESTERN UNION

A. N. WILLIAMS
PRESIDENT

1201 PART I ((44).

The filing time shown in the date line on telegrams and day letters is STANDARD TIME at point of origin. Time of receipt is STANDARD TIME at point of destination

VC59 55 GOVT=WUX WASHINGTON DC 27 333P

MRS GERTRUDE WOOD=

THE FACT OF WAR

ON AV LARAMIE ILL

64 SEP 27 PM 2 46

REGRET TO INFORM YOU YOUR SON WAS SERIOUSLY WOUNDED IN

AND WOUNDING

SS IS

RECEIVED ADRESS WA   ON   QUOTE PRIVATE EDWARD W WOOD

JR SERIAL NUMBER (HOSPITALIZED) CENTRAL POSTAL DIRECTORY

APO 640 C/O POSTMASTER NEW YORK NEW YORK UNQUOTE YOU WILL

BE ADVISED AS REPORTS OF CONDITION ARE RECEIVED=

J A ULIO THE ADJUTANT GENERAL.

FRANCE

SEPTEMBER 1944

SEPTEMBER 1984

It is fitting that I should have entered war here in 1944, the site of the fiercest battle of World War I. Now I understand it for what it really was, the bloodiest, costliest battlefield of that war. From February to December 1916, almost three hundred thousand young men, French and German, were killed or found missing within these forts; over four hundred thousand were wounded, many crippled for life. Here at Douaumont were days and nights, nights and days of waiting for death, a discipline in courage beyond my understanding, a conquest over fear and pain so intense that finally the men who fought in blood broke, and their breaking made the basis for the defeat of France in World War II. Douaumont, where I stand, the first landscape of the world turned into a lunar nightmare, this concrete fort where I stand alone once surrounded by a sea of blood.

Now in shellfire's wilderness nothing grows but trees, a sea of trees stretching to the gray horizon from the rubble of this fort; darkly writhing, wind-driven branches, fed by roots nourished on the skulls, thighs and backbones of three hundred thousand men.

Can nothing rise from blood but trees?

I take my nerve into my raw hands and leave the safety of the fort, the world of tourists. I plunge deep into the dark forest, dwarfed by monstrously high tree trunks. Light above me thickens. The sky disappears. I sink into a tunnel of green and gray and black, lashed by branches swaying in the wind. The air? The air? Does it whimper? For I am told that each year spirits still rise from the land, forced from the earth as if earth cannot accept the burden of our dead. I walk deeper into the forest and wonder if I shall see a dance of skeletons, still clothed in rotting uniforms and holding rusted rifles.

The air cries . . . laughter?

My hands sweat. On sudden impulse, I turn and rush back to the safety of the tourist world.

I stand again on the top of the fort and overlook the tossing trees. The pain, the loss, the lives of men, young men, who should have been lovers, husbands, fathers, men who should have written books, mined coal, danced, drunk beer, sweated, made love, worshiped God . . . three hundred thousand men lost forever in this mighty wound upon the earth.

CHAPTER 1

THE LAND OF THE WOUNDED: ENTRANCE AND EXIT

> *They had crossed a strange line; they had become*
> *wounded men; and everybody realized, including*
> *themselves, dimly, that they were now different. . . .*
> *They had been initiated into a strange, insane,*
> *twilight fraternity where explanation would be*
> *forever impossible. . . . Tenderness was all that*
> *could be given . . .*
> —James Jones, *The Thin Red Line*

SEPTEMBER 1944

To be nineteen years old, to be nineteen and an infantryman, to be nineteen and fight for the liberation of France from the Nazis in the summer of 1944! That time of hot and cloudless blue days when the honeybees buzzed about our heads and we shouted strange phrases in words we did not understand to men and women who cheered us as if we were gods. That summer, that strangely glorious summer when we rushed across France, the Nazis fleeing just ahead of us. *Drive east, drive east.* South of Paris the day it was liberated, across the Marne to Château-Thierry (battlefields of the war in which my father and uncle had fought), then Reims with its cathedral, the most beautiful structure I had ever seen in my life, its magical flying buttresses brilliant against the August sky. Each village we entered started another party for us, as we shared bottles of wine hoarded since 1940 and kisses from wet-mustached men and smooth-cheeked women while we hurled cigarettes and chocolate from our armored half-track and got drunk together and laughed and cried and screamed, for we had freed them from evil. For that glorious moment, the dream of freedom lived and we were ten feet tall.

The essence of that dream and that liberation culminated for me in one day and one night just as the Third Army neared Germany, September 6 and 7, 1944, three months after the invasion. Early that morning, after a predawn firefight in the dense forests along the ridges falling toward the Moselle River, my platoon of the Forty-eighth Armored Infantry Battalion, Seventh Armored Division, XX Corps, freed a small town in Lorraine on our final drive toward the German border. In the dark we drove in column down a long circling road through the steeply pitched mountains. The town lay in a valley above the Moselle, center of a slave labor camp crowded with men and women and children who had been shipped from all countries of Europe to work the region's iron mines for the Nazis.

When we reached the center of the town, the joy of those just liberated bordered on insanity, for, truly, these men and women were mad from their newfound sense of freedom. These people, these French, these Dutch, Belgians, Poles, Italians, had been living in conditions beyond our imagination. Our armored half-track was engulfed by them as they clambered over its steel sides, grabbed us, kissed us. Our eyes were smothered with the gazes of women screaming to make love, to give us their bodies since they had nothing else to give, offering even to bathe us; they touched us, caressed us, stroked our muscles for their size, stared in wonder at the weapons we held, nodded in delight at our strength.

At dawn I had stood on the back of the track with the rest of the squad, the terror of the night, my first experience of combat, still shocking my emotions *the explosion of that firefight, men trying to kill each other with M-1 rifles and machine pistols, blue and yellow holes punching into the night.* But now the faces beneath me were screaming of their freedom and, suddenly, like the rest of my squad, I hurled cigarettes and Hershey bars into the crowd as if to disperse the images of my fear.

The lieutenant came over and ordered us to mount up; we were to drive to the town square through still crowded streets. We parked near an old iron fountain. The square lay open on all sides, a yellow stucco government building dominating one end.

We heard a roar, a confused jumble of shouts and thudding feet out of sight, around the corner. A few young men broke into view, running backwards, staring intently at someone we could not see. A Frenchwoman, no older than I, stumbled into view. The man behind her slammed his fist into her shoulder. She almost fell. The men jeered at her; they continued to hit her shoulders so she could not regain her balance.

The women lining her path toward the center of the square did not give her solace. An old, gray-haired woman, dressed like my Grandma Green in a black smock reaching below her knees, pursed her wrinkled lips and spat. Another reached out and yanked at the woman's arm. A third pulled at the bodice of her flowered dress, exposing the cleft of her breasts.

The men laughed.

Two men behind her pushed the woman through the mob. She stumbled. A small boy ran in front of her and kicked at her feet. She fell. She skidded on the cobblestones. Her extended arm crumpled under her body. She shook her wrist with pain as she clambered to her feet. The men pushed her down again. They grabbed her legs so that her dress blew above her waist. The woman tried to hold it over her white thighs with her hands. The men dragged her over the cobblestones. Her back and buttocks thudded on their rough surface.

The men lifted her twisting body to the top of a small platform hastily erected by the fountain. One man reached inside her dress. There was a particular intensity in his eyes as he pulled out one of her breasts. He stroked it sensuously, his fingers

8

moving over her nipple. Suddenly, his features hardened. His fingernails pinched down into her brown nipple. The woman bit her tongue. She did not cry. Blood reddened her lips and breast simultaneously.

The man ripped away the rest of her dress. She hid her face with clenched hands, her body obscenely white in the early morning sun. She tried to cross her legs to hide the small patch of brown hair at the crotch. Each time she moved, the man who mocked her made a great show of lifting the offending leg and putting it beside the other, even spreading her legs so that the lips of her vagina were open to the crowd. He reached down and lifted her with his arms. He forced her to pirouette before them as if she were a model.

"Jesus H. Christ!" the sergeant muttered.

The crowd shouted its approval. All eyes centered on the naked figure now slumped before them on the platform. Her body still, her head bowed, the seated woman cried quietly, tears wetting her face.

The man over her took a straightedge razor from his pocket. He opened it, thumbed the blade. With his free hand he reached down and curled her thick, blond hair into strands. He slowly, almost like a lover, coiled a braid around his fingers. Suddenly, he yanked it so tight her head moved. He lifted the braid high above her head, raised the razor, swung the gleaming blade so close to her scalp it nicked her skin.

Again.

Again.

Again.

Each time, with slow methodical movements, the razor flashed toward her head, like a scythe swinging over a field of rippling wheat.

Blood dripped down the woman's scalp. She licked it from her face with her lips, salt tears and salt blood the bitter elixir of her flesh.

When the man finished cropping her head, he took a bowl of water and a bar of soap. He made a great flourish of soaping his hands until they were lathered white. He rubbed the soap briskly into her blood-streaming scalp.

She winced.

A man in the crowd yelled his objection. He had seen enough.

But the barber continued shaving the woman's head.

He scraped his razor expertly over her lathered scalp. He shaved it until she was completely bald. When he finished, he grabbed her chin and twisted her face toward his. He glared down at her for a long, long moment, and it was odd, for I thought I saw his eyes moisten with sudden tears.

Then he held a mirror to her features. She grimaced, almost a comical expression. Her lips puckered. She spat. *La femme scalpée* spat up into his face.

He swung his arm. Her head snapped back. He started to swing again.

Someone in our squad screamed: "STOP IT! STOP IT, YA SONSABITCHES!" He fired a long burst into the air from the .50-caliber machine gun at the front of the half-track.

The crowd swung toward it. The woman slipped from the platform to the cobblestones and disappeared into a store on the square. The sergeant shrugged his shoulders.

The lieutenant came over to the track. He told us to mount up. We were moving out.

We had liberated the town from the Nazis.

It had taken five weeks for the XX Corps to begin this final thrust into Germany. In that time Patton's Third Army ("Old Blood and Guts" they called him; we responded, "our blood and his guts"), treating armored troops as cavalry, had swept three hundred miles across France and liberated over thirty thousand square miles of French territory. Chaos rode the countryside as Germans fled, Americans pursued, and the Resistance killed Nazi collaborators and celebrated freedom. As a replacement into the Seventh Armored Division, I and thirty or forty other casuals had spent much of that month searching for the division so we could join it.

Always just a few days behind combat, we had seen the consequences of that freedom: instant joy mingled with fierce revenge and terror. We traveled across France that strangely glorious summer, always hearing that the Seventh Armored Division and the XX Corps lay just ahead *drive east, drive east, drive east!* as we entered those towns on hot and cloudless blue days when honeybees buzzed all around us.

I remember the eggs we bartered for and boiled on our gasoline stoves; the encampment in the forests of Fontainebleau, where I saw my first air raid and tracers scarring the night; the long-haired blonde of sixteen or so who bicycled by our roadblock one day as the man next to me muttered, "Fuck her, fuck her," seeing the fear on the girl's features, the acceptance of her certain destiny of rape tight upon her face; the second lieutenant who went AWOL just south of Paris, returning two days later with odd-looking paintings he said with great glee were done by a man called Picasso (whom I had never heard of in my youth and childhood!); the Free French Forces with their little cars and little shorts and tanned legs and little pistols that shot real bullets; the drunken driver who knocked down a house while turning his tank in the middle of the street. All of it a movie in which I played JohnWayneHumphreyBogartGaryCooper—like Hemingway, a hero of battle.

It *was* a movie at first, an endless spectacle. I remember one afternoon sitting by myself on a hillside, watching an army move along the road below me: trucks, tanks, jeeps, dust, men shouting, gesticulating, cursing. An army of men beneath me, in pursuit of our enemy. And overhead the planes: bombers in great silver phalanxes, pursuit planes above them. Sometimes at night came the ruthless trajectory of antiaircraft fire, sometimes the wailing, whistling murmur of distant bombs. We drove through it—like being in a dream of all the wars and battles buried in my blood memory as a boy of the deepest South: Marathon and Salamis and Agincourt and Waterloo and Bull Run and Gettysburg and the Wilderness and the Alamo, San Juan Hill, Saint-Mihiel, the Meuse-Argonne, Verdun, the Somme. Wars of my childhood inheritance.

The French cheering us on! Liberation!

Oh, to help free a people! To be thanked for the risk! A moment in history so pure, so poignant that it was almost beyond belief: freeing France from the Nazis. And I was lucky enough to be part of it.

I joined the division on the fifth of September in Verdun, where it, along with the entire Third Army, had run out of gas. Armored vehicles and infantrymen were sprawled across the countryside, unable to move, while the Germans slowly regrouped as they fled back toward the Moselle River. We bivouacked in old French forts from World War I, site of that bloodiest battle: seven hundred thousand young men killed or wounded or missing in less than nine months. The plain spreading beneath those forts harbored memories of hundreds of years of warfare, since the time of ancient Rome.

For me, this was the conclusion of a journey that had started when I, a boy of eighteen, volunteered to serve in combat as an infantryman with all the other children of the Western world, believing then, knowing then, that the dream of peace and justice and equity for all, the dream of my mother's populist forebears in Alabama, could be won only from victory in war: defeating the Nazis and the Japanese who threatened the democracy and the country I loved.

And yet . . . ? The image of that woman with her shorn hair, spitting up into the Frenchman's arrogant face, bothered me: was this the freedom for which we fought, to immediately turn on others weaker than ourselves?

As a replacement into the squad, I was too terrified and alone to speak of my concern to the men around me, sensing how they regarded me—a stranger, untested in the enterprise of killing and wounding. How I longed for a companion, a friend, one of those with whom I had traveled across France, crossed the Atlantic on a troop ship, trained with in the United States, buddied with in high school. But all I met was cold reserve that day and night as we waited for the thrust toward Germany to begin.

The division, the XX Corps, the whole Third Army brooded while we spread out over the hills of Lorraine, waiting for gas to flow so that fighting could be renewed. Our generals argued over priorities between the First and Third Armies, British and Americans . . . while we sat and waited and smoked.

The next morning, the sixth of September, we left the line of departure, knifing toward the city of Metz, site of a great battle in the Franco-Prussian War of 1870.

My loneliness, my sense of alienation, intensified as the members of the squad took their regular seats on the half-track in which we would roll toward Germany. Their words and laughter poured over me, around me, under me. Until I proved myself in combat, I simply did not exist. I had been told by fellow replacements at the repple-depple that this was the way I would be treated when I joined the squad. Replacements knew no one as their friends. Sometimes they were even given the tasks of greatest danger as guinea pigs, targets of opportunity, while the rest of the squad crouched in greater security.

Meat for the butcher.

We rolled toward the Moselle that morning, stopping only when great tanks at our side fired their artillery pieces high above barren hills. I marveled at the peasants who came up to the tanks and methodically seized empty shell casings (so they could later sell the brass), seemingly oblivious to German fire.

Twice we dismounted. Once at a rumor of poison gas. Then to penetrate a French village—a high brick wall at our side, five yards between each man, alert for the hand grenade that might come lobbing over the wall. At the edge of the village, we halted in the ditch at the side of the road.

"Put on those fuckin' bayonets!" the sergeant said when he ran back from crouching at the lieutenant's side. "We gonna cross the road and clean those motherfuckers outta that house behind the wall."

My fingers trembled as I fastened my bayonet to the end of my rifle.

We ran in little groups across the road and ducked behind the wall. Nothing happened. The Germans had fled.

My bayonet jammed when I tried to remove it from my rifle. The soldier seated on the ground next to me pulled it free, glaring at me with contempt.

Somewhere later that afternoon, north and west of Metz, the track halted near a road sign to Luxembourg. We lay behind it while shells from a German 88-millimeter artillery piece smashed into a farmhouse across the road. (The explosions lacked all the drama of a shelling in a movie; rather, they looked like dirty backfires from an old car.) We retreated back down the highway as a tank joined us.

At dusk we dismounted from the half-track. We walked at the side of the tank. Once we stopped, and the lieutenant talked fiercely to a Frenchman who then motioned us down a darkened side road, its trees forming great menacing arches above our heads. We moved warily into a forest where fog slipped through black branches and rain dripped from sodden leaves. As we penetrated deeper into that darkness, gravel suddenly splattered my leggings, stinging me. The pavement in front of me exploded with an orange burst of fire; a blue hole cut into the fog ahead. I scrambled toward the ditch, crawling on my hands and knees like a terrified animal.

The spectacle had just ended, the movie choreographed by Hemingway, starring John and Gary and Humphrey. I was no longer an observer; I was suddenly, instantly, peeingly, playing a part in it: SOMEONE OUT THERE WANTED ME DEAD, little ol' Eddie Wood, his momma's boy, dead!

I buried myself in the ditch, branches snapping above my head.

"WHO THE FUCK IS THAT?" the soldier behind me cried.

My teeth chattered so I could not speak.

"I goddamn near shot ya. Be quiet, for Chris' sake."

The lieutenant fired over our heads at a blur that suddenly popped up from the ditch ahead of us and ran; the silhouette sprawled back upon the road, its rifle clattering to the black pavement.

The lieutenant hesitated. He waved us ahead. I walked by the dead German, a boy no older than I, his blond hair plastered to his face with rain.

Whenever the lieutenant crossed a culvert, he leaned over and fired bursts from his machine gun into the opening. I shuddered, imagining myself trapped in a tunnel beneath the ground, bullets slamming from the concrete, shredding my unprotected flesh.

At dawn we stopped, mounted the track again. We entered another town, its streets deserted. The signs were in German. Nobody visible. Nobody. As if all human beings had disappeared. Shutters on the buildings slammed in the early morning wind. We parked in the middle of the square. Shells whispered over our heads, tearing through the gray sky. They should have been the ducks I shot with my father as a boy.

We left the village with its closed shutters and doors. The road swung to our left, then our right, a ninety-degree turn. We could not see around the corner.

The lieutenant and the sergeant dismounted. The soldier who had cursed me in the dark the night before jumped from the track. He shouted to the lieutenant, then pointed up at me, glaring ferociously. The lieutenant slowly calmed him, then jerked his arm at our squad. I clambered from the half-track with the other men, my rifle awkward in my arms. As we started around the curve in the road, expecting enemy fire at any moment, my mouth could not form words, my breath seemed louder than any shellfire. I hugged the ditch at the side of the road. When nothing happened, I stepped from the shrubs to the macadam pavement. The air was still. Fog hovered around the trees, masking the mansard roof of a French farmhouse that towered above the poplars to my right. For that moment, that small moment in time, though I did not know it, we were in front of the whole Third Army. The Germans had fallen back across the Moselle River ahead to regroup.

Up the road I could just distinguish the outline of a bridge. I walked toward it. With each faltering step I seemed to penetrate a great vaulted tomb of silence, a silence never known or experienced before—as if all time and motion had ceased and I was the only living being in the universe. This was the silence I had encountered the day I first joined the men of the division—their refusal to help the stranger, the replacement, until he had proven himself under fire. Men did not support each other in comradeship as they did in all those movies I had seen. They entered a place of intense stillness where each lived alone in terror of immediate death. The silence deepened, hovering about me, palpable, almost as if I must soon slip into it and sink into eternity.

I sank to my knees when the lieutenant joined us. I could not speak, my throat constricted with fear.

Just ahead of us, on our side of the river, west of the Moselle, lay a barge canal twenty or thirty yards wide. Before retreating, the Germans had blown a bridge spanning it. Made of steel I-beams, the bridge had broken apart at the explosion and jackknifed into the green water of the canal, forming a V. Gingerly, we clambered down one side, holding the steel trusses with one hand, our rifles with the other. I feared I might be shot and tumble, helpless, into the canal. The gap between the two sets of trusses, just before they penetrated the water, was two or three yards. I tensed my legs. Jumped. One foot swung into the water. I yanked it up, climbed the slippery steel to the other bank. The lieutenant joined us there.

We stood beneath the abutment on the other side of the bridge. A machine gun fired, its bullets whining off the concrete. The lieutenant gentled us as if we were wild animals. He motioned us to the top of the abutment when the machine gun stopped its chattering.

In the distance, several hundred yards to our left, I could see another bridge, much longer, rising out of the mist over the Moselle. Little figures of men ran up the abutment.

"Fire, goddamn it!" the lieutenant cried. "Fire!"

I threw my rifle to my shoulder, settled on a running silhouette. I led it as I did the quail I had shot as a boy. I started to pull the trigger. The bridge exploded like a concrete geyser:

rubble and steel and smoke hid the man at whom I aimed. I fired into the haze.

"Shit!" the lieutenant cursed. "We'll have to cross the fucking river in boats now."

He motioned us back down the slope and across the canal, not knowing we were the forward contingent of the whole Third Army.

The bank of the canal offered us protection from enemy fire. Our tanks were ranged below it. We dropped, exhausted, at the forward lip of the bank. The tanks fired over the rise.

I rolled over on my back and looked down the hill.

A great plain lay behind me. Though it was misty and gray, I could see for miles. The road was lined with tanks and trucks and half-tracks and jeeps and men who stood in little clumps like ants. Airplanes, small artillery spotters, buzzed overhead. Dirty smoke from shellfire drifted over the road and hid it for an instant like dark mist following a heavy rain. Men shouted at each other, gesticulated; I could not hear their words. The air snapped with the shriek of lightning.

One of the men who had crossed the canal with me stood at the bottom of the hill. He yelled commands to a mortar squad firing at a group of apartment buildings, just this side of the Moselle. A dirty puff of smoke suddenly exploded at his side. He spun as if a giant had slammed him in the shoulder, bouncing off the ground as he fell. A medic ran to him where he flopped up and down like a chicken with its head cut off, spurting blood from his arm.

Another puff of smoke dirtied the air. A piece of shrapnel slammed into the earth at my side. The grass around it curled.

The lieutenant made hand signals to us to assemble at a stand of trees farther back, near the road that led to the farmhouse. I grabbed a box of .30-caliber machine gun ammunition and ran, understanding, for the first time, how to survive here: live for the moment. Don't think about the near future, not even the next few minutes.

We started to dig foxholes under the trees. I hit a root almost immediately. I struck furiously at it, using the edge of my metal entrenching tool as an ax. The blade was too dull; the root would not snap. At any moment I was sure another artillery shell would split the air above me, send hot shrapnel tearing into my flesh. I frantically slammed at the pulpy mass. My breath was choked. I could not breathe. Sweat poured from my face, though a cold September mist drifted through the grove of trees.

The men at my side had their holes half dug. They had moved farther out from the tree trunk where the roots were smaller. I scrambled over the ground to their side. No one spoke to me.

I started to dig. My blade met no roots. The shovel pierced the deep black earth, the sweet earth in which I would soon hide... and then, then, the slam of a sledgehammer lifted me high and I whirled up and up and up through a tunnel of green leaves toward the sky, my hands extended as if to grasp those leaves and the dark brown limbs rushing by me, halting my flight into eternity. My fingers brushed over them. They would not hold.

I flew higher into the sky and seemed to merge with the clouds, mix with their wispy tendrils, not knowing whether to continue this arc toward eternity or fall back to the sweet, sweet earth. With a falling, sliding swoop I tumbled out of the sky. Fell to my knees. I put my fingers up to my face. Blood, thick and red and dark, swiftly pumping, covered them. I reached up and touched my head. My helmet was gone. Blood poured from a hole on the left side of my skull. A hard lump protruded from my torn scalp. A piece of shrapnel was embedded in the bone. I looked behind me. My pants were ripped away, my right buttock was blown open. Beneath the yellow-white fat, I could see the raw, red meat, like the steaks my father had once fed me.

"Hold still, Wood! Hold still!" the medic cried, blood from the tip of his wounded nose spraying my face. "Stop wiggling, goddamnit! I gotta get this morphine in ya." The blood from his own wound sprinkled over me like spittle from a dying sneeze.

As he poked at my arm, I heard the whisper of the shells above me and wondered why their sigh sounded like the wings of the ducks my father and I had once shot in Mississippi bayous. Not yet in pain, I lay there, loose-jointed, until they tumbled me into a stretcher and ran with me toward the ambulance parked on the macadam road near the grove of trees. Once they dropped me, leaving me helpless, as an artillery shell slammed too close. I stared up at them as they hovered in the lee of the ambulance, their place of sanctuary.

When the shelling stopped, they lifted me into the ambulance.

"You didn't like it much up here, did you, Wood?" the lieutenant asked as they slammed the door.

My journey into the land of the wounded began in that ambulance after one day of combat, before I had proven myself, those men in arms still uncertain of my courage and my strength, the lieutenant's words my epitaph.

Being moved by ambulance from Battalion Aid Station into World War I bunkers, I smelled the cloying odor of blood, feeling it drip on me from the stretcher above. Here at the front, before there were forms and bureaucrats to describe and fasten to me some categories of wound and pain, I touched men who, for an instant, cared for me with greater compassion than I had ever experienced at any time or place in my life—men who lit my cigarette and held it in their fingers while I puffed, men who returned to me again and again, seeing if my paralyzed hand would yet move, if my bowels were free, my urine not pink with blood, murmuring to me gently, even crying. I remember one boy my age who had ridden to the front with me, weeping as he cut off my bloody clothes in Battalion Aid Station. I remember the soldier I had watched being wounded visiting me in the field hospital, his arm still bloody in its sling, offering me a package of cigarettes.

Gentleness and compassion, a softness so difficult for

the American male to express—always there but held back, contained by some impenetrable shell, breaking open now and warming me after I was wounded, as if love could be given only within the frame of violence and one must be expressed in conjunction with the other. The language of war and peace, violence and love, hate and compassion that I have sought to understand on my journey through the land of the wounded.

* * *

SEPTEMBER 1984

Icelandic Airlines
New York/Luxembourg

> *For forty years I have traveled through this strange land of the wounded, haunted by memories of that day in combat, that terrain between Verdun and the Moselle River over which we lumbered in armored vehicles. Now I return to the place of my wounding, in search of the final meaning of my journey. I pierce the final trajectory of my life and time. Last week, before I left Cape Cod for France, I read the letters of my youth in the Army: spring, summer, fall of 1944. Dad saved them for me, a gift most deeply appreciated.*
> *Flying above this great ocean, the one over which I moved in a troop ship at age nineteen, I tick off the track through time that young boy followed as he began his own flight toward the Canal des Mines in September 1944: April 7, leaving pre-med school at UCLA for Camp Hood, Oregon; April 20, a troop train to Kansas; early June, maneuvers; middle June, ten days of furlough, five spent on my canoe trip with Dad in Quetico, our last gesture of love; early July, a troop train to Fort Meade. The wheel of time spinning faster and faster, whipping me toward that rendezvous with my wounding. August 3, the troop ship to England; August 13,*

landing in Liverpool; August 17, beginning that wild journey across France, the wheel turning faster, faster . . .

And now, as I fly across the Atlantic, piercing time, I sense those two trajectories—one, that youth's, that boy's (still a child); the other, mine today, forty years later, this man so alone, so uncertain, having rejected the tools of war, his father's rifle. The track of his youth and childhood speeding faster, the dream, the land, the family and the flesh still pristine and pure in his heart and body, living in an era before these jets, these vast systems of communication, computers, television, a time before these atomic bombs, a time when Russia was still our ally, when we possessed a common enemy, a time of far greater simplicity, and in the oddest kind of way, less fear. Two trajectories speeding toward the banks of the Moselle River, mine now of age and uncertainty, his my son, my father his of youth and utopia . . .

September 6, 1984
North of Metz

Nothing is familiar.
I search and search and search.
I wander through great centers of iron and steel mills, remembering nothing. I drive a great expressway built through this valley: no landmarks, no symbols seem the same. Is it all gone? Eradicated?
Perhaps this whole trip was an act of madness? An old man in his dotage unable to come to terms with the real conditions of his life?

September 7, 1984
Canal des Mines
Talange, France

But I try once again. And at noon today the two trajectories meet . . .

The water of the canal is as green as I remember it. Though rebuilt since the war, the bridges over it are the same—steel-trussed, heavy, solid, firm. Behind me I see that great valley of memory where forty years ago an army moved, different now, expresswayed, industrialized. Still, reality and my memory are so similar. The hills down which we fought that night rise in the distance, even the weather today is much the same, a slight mist, drifting rain, the lifting and falling of the clouds, a cold chill in the air. And there to my left is the French farmhouse I remember, its mansard roof rising above the trees.

I stand on the bank of the canal and remember the broken trusses down which that boy clambered. I hear the distant chatter of a machine gun again, the soft pop of a mortar. That boy of nineteen works his way down the truss, swings his foot, leaps across the open water. The machine gun fires again. Bullets whine as they ricochet off the concrete abutment into the canal.

I watch him. I know him. I feel him.

The trajectories of time begin to merge and suddenly I am filled with fierce, exultant pride. That boy, that boy my father, my son a stranger to all men around him, so afraid and so alone but crossing this canal under fire. The courage.

I know him. I admire him. I love him.

I sense his fear and his terror: Mama, Mama, they'll kill me, Mama. Mama, Mama, I want your breasts. These men, they do not talk to me, they ignore me. I am so alone, Mama. Afraid. So afraid. But must not show my fear.

Oh, my son, my child, my father and myself.

Oh, my son, my child, my father and myself.

I weep now. I weep great salten tears for him, for all those years to come, his journey into the land of the wounded, a hole in his head and half an ass, scars soon to be cut forever into his flesh.

I weep for my son, my child, my father and myself. Tears not of pain but of sudden fierce exultation as I watch him dig his foxhole under that great tree in the terrible silence which is war. I am filled with a terrible and fierce pride for that boy, terrified, yet still doing what was required, alone, sent into this cauldron totally alone.

I weep for him, for all the boys of his generation, eighteen and nineteen, all the boys of my generation, of my father's time, boys of all those wars: Marathon, Salamis, Agincourt, Waterloo, Bull Run, Gettysburg, the Alamo, San Juan Hill, Saint-Mihiel, Meuse-Argonne, Verdun, the Bulge, Chosin Reservoir, Tet. Hot tears of rage and pride as I watch him raise his shovel, strike the sudden root. The field of killing and wounding, his blood, my blood soon to fertilize French soil, dark and red, thick-pumping. I watch him stare at the other men, then slide backwards just to the edge of the circle made by the arching trees. I start to shout: NO AND NO AND NO AND NO. Stay, my child. Do not move. I cannot speak. I shiver. The German gunner jerks the lanyard on his 88-millimeter piece across the river. I shudder. I scream as the shell arcs high above the canal.

The shell bursts above the boy's head. His body slams into the air, twisted, crumpled by the blast, a dirty piece of garbage flung into the branches.

My son, my child, my son, my father, I cry as we merge. We arch up into the sky together, up and up and up into the tunnel of leaves, rising toward all eternity—then suddenly we slide backwards and sink into the darkly bloodied earth.

I slowly rise from this, my place of wounding, the boy and I united again, and I reach up and feel the hole in my head, touch the mighty scar upon my rear, evidence of these forty years.

PART II

THE CAUSES OF WAR
AND WOUNDING

NEW ENGLAND
THE DEEP SOUTH

1637–1942

CHAPTER 2

THE RIFLES OF MY FATHERS

The shadows are lengthening for me. The twilight is here. My days of old have vanished, tone and tint; they have gone glimmering through the dreams of things that were. Their memory is one of wondrous beauty, watered by tears, and coaxed and caressed by the smiles of yesterday. I listen vainly, but with thirsty ear, for the witching melody of faint bugles blowing reveille, of far drums beating the long roll. In my dreams I hear again the crash of guns, the rattle of musketry, the strange, mournful mutter of the battlefield. But in the evening of my memory, I always come back to West Point. Always there echoes and re-echoes in my ears— Duty, Honor, Country. Today marks my final roll call with you. But I want you to know that when I cross the river my last conscious thoughts will be of the Corps; and the Corps; and the Corps. I bid you farewell.
—General Douglas MacArthur,
Farewell Speech to West Point

In September 1972, almost thirty years after I was wounded, my father died. His death marked the end of an era in my life, symbolized by my inheritance, memorabilia of three hundred years of an American family. The most important item in all that vast estate was his rifle, the .30-06 Winchester rifle I had admired so much as a boy. The day after his funeral I found it in the back of his closet, tucked behind his old hunting jacket. I reached around his tweed coats, hefted the rifle's burnished stock and slipped it from the darkness. Its blue steel barrel gleamed dully in the late afternoon light. Its solid weight sagged heavily in my hand. Grief I had repressed during the airplane flight from Boston to the Gulf Coast of Mississippi, through the funeral and the condolences of those half-remembered relatives, exploded in my mind.

I saw Dad again, alive and vital and dominating as he stood by our garage on a cold morning in deer season, his rumpled canvas jacket slung over his shoulders. He slid his rifle from its leather case and lovingly caressed its stock. The walnut surface gleamed beneath his brown-spotted fingers. He winked at me, shook his heavy belly a little, then stepped into his new Oldsmobile and started the four-hundred-mile drive to West Texas, where he and my uncle would hunt for deer on those scrubby and waterless plains.

I did not sleep much until he returned.

Then in the darkness outside my bedroom window (I can remember how cold the glass was to my nose), the flashlights piercing the pitch-black night over the driveway below seemed like beams held in the hands of giants. The two deer, sprawled on top of the car, blood still red-stained upon their nostrils, were both great dragons slain by more than mortal men and soft furry animals I loved for their liquid eyes and supple flesh.

Later that night he and his friends, their bodies still sweaty from the four-day hunt, sat in the kitchen with the door closed against my mother's contempt for their drinking. They shouted, boasted, bragged (and later some would puke) as they recalled their youth, when the deer were much larger and their shots far more precise. I sat in the corner and watched Dad dominate the group—his stories outrageous, his voice raucous, his laughter contagious, his glass filled with what must have been bootleg gin—as he told of the time he had once killed two wild turkeys with one shot, his exploits as a pilot in World War I, how he flew the mail in 1919.

The memory of those days and nights, long forgotten, deeply buried for over thirty years, slammed into my subconscious like the shrapnel of my wounding; those repressed years of love for my father cut into my mind instead of pain and blood . . . the hunting trips before the war when he taught me to shoot, first rabbits, then quail; winter weekends fishing for largemouth bass among the hyacinths on the St. John's River in Florida; summer canoe trips in Canada north of Ely, Minnesota, where we cast into the rocky shoals for smallmouth bass, northern pike and walleye; August months on the Gulf Coast of Alabama and Mississippi, where we fished for specks and red snappers, always more oysters and shrimp than one could eat. And Dad spending money as if it were water, the finest hotels, the best food, the most powerful cars, hand-tailored suits and ties, the latest gadgets, no end to incessant acquisition, his home a sprawl of furniture, antiques, rifles, shotguns, shells, shelf after shelf of Meissen and Spode and Haviland, fishing rods (twenty-two at his death), family papers of three hundred years mixed with canceled checks a month old. Dad roared in and out of that mess like a great tornado, bringing, on sudden impulse, ten and twelve and twenty people for dinner, stirring up the debris of conversation, his great laugh booming irrepressibly.

He swirled around my mother—and how I marveled as she stared up at him, never intimidated by his force. Her Bible, her church, her tithes were her support, a far different world from his. All her money went to charity. Every poor man in the small southern towns in which we lived knew where to obtain a meal or some ready cash. She neither drank nor smoked. Her morality was Calvin's before the nineteenth century corrupted it. Each night was prayer. We blessed our food. Sunday was God's day. Church at eleven and church at seven and silence and prayer in between.

I remember those hours upon our pew, my father leaning forward to wink at some friend as the minister mispronounced a word, my mother holding her hymnal to her breasts, her voice a gentle murmur in my ear:

> *We gather together to face the Lord Jesus*
> *Who hastens and chastens . . .*

Yet the differences between the two, the seldom-expressed rage, the just-repressed tears, the startling contrasts between their masculinity and femininity, were unbearable for that small and only child. I enlisted in the Army four months after I was eighteen and never really returned to them, even after I was wounded in France in 1944, except for a few days of vacation duty which depressed me each year, beginning in the late 1950s after my children were born.

With Dad's death, his rifle so solid in my hands, the family memories of youth and childhood soared vividly to life, especially our summers on the Gulf Coast, when my father's family gathered at Coden and Bayou la Batre for August. Cousins, kissing cousins and cousins once removed, aunts and uncles, grandmothers and grandfathers descended from Texas, Alabama, Mississippi, and we piled red steaming gumbo on our plates, broke crab claws, cavorted while Dad pranced around the table singing:

> *Pharoah and his army got drowned*
> *Now, Mary, don't you weep . . .*

He shouted out the words as he led us to the feast.

I remember Dad with the rudder of our old and barely floatable motorboat in his hands as he called to me, his belly brown and bulging hard above his belt, a shout of joy on his lips as he pointed to the school of speckled trout, white-flashing streaks in the blue sea beneath the red lead keel. Dad would make coffee on the old iron stove in the early morning before dawn. We drank it thick with sugar, harsh with chicory.

We would motor out of the harbor just as the sun began to rise, the sea flat green beneath a pearl-gray sky. I could see the islands, a dark line on the horizon, slowly grow in size, almost as if they rose by their own volition from the mysterious sea. When the wind came up, the bow slammed into the waves. I sometimes took the tiller as Dad readied our bamboo poles.

We would anchor between the islands, near the old, rusted iron pipe that rose from the Mississippi Sound. The pipe, jutting straight up from the sea bed, was all that remained of an island destroyed by a hurricane thirty years before. From its rusted mouth a stream of sweet artesian water still bubbled, glistening in the hard glare of the summer sun. It splashed into the salten sea as it had in those halcyon days when excursion boats brought summer folks from New Orleans and Mobile to the long wooden wharf next to the old hotel where they spent their nights and days.

I would marvel at that pipe as we sat and rocked to the swaying of the sea, our poles cast down upon the deck. Dad told me tales of his childhood when he sailed out to the islands, attended parties on the hotel veranda just beyond the old dock, flirted with the girls, even drank water from this very pipe where we now moored, somnolent in the rhythm of the sea . . .

Oh, I remember that spring rising from the sea and the sun hot above our heads and the bow of the boat rising with each long-hissing wave, driven by the southern wind.

I remember those days and nights after his funeral, when I returned north and walked down Massachusetts Avenue in Cambridge to my job in the Planning Department at the Massachusetts Institute of Technology, past Harvard Square and Central Square, past those bookstores, those intent young men and women rushing to classes, rushing to appointments, clutching their precious notebooks to their breasts.

I remember him in this world so alien to all he had been, as if this rifle held so tightly in my hands, its blue steel barrel, its walnut stock, contained the best memories of the past. Manhood: symbolized by this weapon, so heavy, so solid in my hands, shimmering with symbols of that lost childhood, this rifle of my fathers, my inheritance, the form and content of who I was and who I was meant to be . . .

Our home was always full of guns and weapons: slingshots, BB guns, pellet guns, .22-caliber rifles, .30-06 rifles, 10- and 12- and 20-gauge shotguns, sawed-off shotguns, pistols—the arsenal of most southern homes. I was fascinated by all the memorabilia Dad had collected during his years as an Air Service pilot in World War I: his uniform, his campaign hat, his cavalry boots with spurs (airplanes then had the same romantic quality as horses), an old French 75-millimeter shell my uncle brought home from Europe after World War I, pictures of Dad's airplane in flight, and the tip of the propeller of that plane, sawed off after he cracked up in 1918.

When I was very young, in the early 1930s, an air circus visited those towns throughout the South in which we lived. Dad knew everyone who flew then; it remained that small a fraternity. He introduced me to men who one day would be famous: Wiley Post, he of the eye patch, killed with Will Rogers in Alaska in 1936; Eddie Stinson, builder of the best airplanes then, who gave me my first ride in a Stinson monoplane in 1929 or so. It was at the air circus that I saw my first crash, as a plane spun out of control and slammed into the ground a hundred yards from the grandstand where we sat. The pilot crawled from the wreckage and everyone cheered wildly. That night, a cast on his broken arm, he came to our home with all the other pilots and their lady friends. I crept from my upstairs bed, seated myself on the top of the stairs, heard raucous shouts, cries, tipsy laughter, boasting, Dad's voice always overwhelming the others as he poured out his bootleg gin.

My mother sat in the corner alone, knitting, her lips pursed with disdain.

When my father saw me through the railing, he pushed his way through the mass of friends and took me in his arms. He lifted me high above his head, his ruby lips glistening, mouth half-open, as he spun me around the room, a dance of his own, his laughter joyous in my ears.

"My son!" he cried. "My son! Someday he'll fly. He... why he'll fly to the moon. Better'n any of us... Eddie! Eddie! Eddie!"

He spun me out of doors when we heard the buzz of an airplane motor. Others followed. We listened intently. Out of the distance, out of the night, out of those fervid stars pressed deep into velvet southern sky, air warm with a tropical breeze, out of that night came another Stinson monoplane, like the one we had flown earlier in the day. It dropped toward our house. Lower. Lower. Its wings wagged drunkenly. A figure leaned out of the plane's window. Waved. Waved again. The plane dipped low, almost out of control, then lurched around in a huge circle, swinging about the second story of the house.

"That's Stinson," a voice murmured. "Drunk as a skunk again . . . "

"He'll kill himself one day . . . "

The plane buzzed lower, shot up into the night.

My father hugged me closer to his broad chest.

This, then, my father's legacy: his rifle, his romantic tales of life as a pilot in World War I, his love of nature expressed in hunting and fishing, his success in business—all evidence of his vibrant masculinity, the masculinity he demanded of me and in which he gave me early training.

I do not remember when he gave me my first weapon. I have at home a pistol carved of wood which I must have received at five or six; at its side lies an old Crossman air pistol given to me a year or two later, followed, of course, by a BB gun, a .22 rifle, then a .410-gauge shotgun.

I killed my first bird with a BB gun at my aunt's farm in King William, Virginia. Robert Henry, a black youth, looked after me when I was there. He and I were in the vegetable garden, shooting at tin cans. English sparrows—at least, I believe they were—hopped in the fruit trees at the border to the garden.

Robert Henry teased me, saying I could not hit a bird. I feared he was right.

He taunted me again.

In sudden anger I threw up my gun and aimed at a singing sparrow.

The moment I pulled the trigger, the sparrow halted its song. Dust puffed from its chest where the pellet struck it. It spasmed. Spun. Clung to its branch upside down. Hung there, swinging, for what seemed an eternity. Its claws slipped. It swung by one foot, let go, thudded to the hard earth.

When I picked it up, a drop of blood from its bill reddened my nail. I almost puked.

I always felt nauseated when I killed. I remember a rabbit frozen with fear in a stubbled cornfield. It had become disoriented in its flight from my father, who was behind me; it stopped not ten feet away, brown ears twitching, blood in its veins pinkly visible beneath its pulsing skin.

"Shoot it! Shoot it, Eddie!" Dad cried from behind me. "Kill it, boy!"

The rabbit's head burst open when I pulled the trigger of the shotgun. I picked up its broken, bleeding body and loathed it, almost as if I wanted to kill it again.

"Good shooting, son," Dad called. "You didn't mess up the meat."

He took me pheasant hunting in Nebraska one fall before the war. The birds were so plentiful that any swale held fifteen or twenty. They fluttered up like great chickens and were that easy to shoot. Once, my shot did not immediately kill the bird. It plummeted, broken-winged, into the brown, dry prairie grass. I seized the bird by its hard, black legs, put my foot on its neck, its dark eyes staring up at me. I yanked its feet. The head stayed under my boot. The bleeding neck, obscenely protruding from green-glistening feathers, pumped blood dark upon the grass.

I hunted even harder. In the summers when we went on our fishing trips into the Gulf, I always took my .22 rifle. Dad, of course, carried his .410 sawed-off shotgun. I shot gulls with the .22. I got so I could hit them, even at thirty or forty yards, sometimes almost impossible shots. The birds fell from the blue sky, from freewheeling silhouettes to squawking piles of feathers on the sea, to disappear in the swirl of a feeding shark.

Dad taught me what it meant to be a man in the Deep South of the 1930s.

D ad's .30-06 Winchester rifle symbolized his masculine mystique, a silent language speaking of what a man must be. A man must be able to use a rifle to defend himself, those he loved, those weak and dependent, women and children, those who sought liberty. Killing one's enemies was the path to freedom.

With the system of masculine beliefs that Dad willed me came an enormous and complex pattern of individual and social activities, ranging from the fellowship of the rifle—the men with whom one hunted—to respect for its technology and killing power: cleaning it properly, caring for it, "zeroing" it in for accuracy. These activities formed my passage to maturity. The Winchester is threaded through my childhood memories as if being a man could not be separated from owning and using a weapon.

When Dad was a child in Moss Point, Mississippi, in the 1890s, the Civil War was only thirty years away, both slavery and the frontier still a vibrant family memory. His father had been born in 1869 in Marshall, Illinois, on my grandparents' migration from Massachusetts to Mississippi. In that time and place, owning and using a rifle was essential to survival. Squirrels and rabbits, deer and possum, quail and turkeys were shot for food, animal meat salted away for the winter. In fact, Dad once told me that in the winter of 1904 or 1905 his people even shot robins so the family wouldn't starve. "Mighty good eating, Eddie," he said with a grin.

Dad was a tenth-generation male born into that pioneer world. Ten generations of his male ancestors had successfully dominated the dark and primitive killing grounds of the American frontier, beginning with the first settler, Thomas Lumbert, who moved to Cape Cod from Dorchester and Scituate in 1637, opening the first tavern, or "ordinary," in Barnstable on the Cape. Ten generations of men carried their weapons as they overwhelmed their enemies in this dark and unknown land—my inheritance of rifles and violence buried deep in the American past.

It was my family history of wars and woundings that led me to volunteer for the infantry in France. There was tradition in the rifles of all those male ancestors, the weapons each generation used in the conquest of the land: the seventeenth-century wheel-lock and matchlock muskets that Thomas Lumbert carried as he fled England and the repression of Charles I; the same weapons used by the Puritans in their destruction of the Pequot Indians on the banks of the Mystic River in 1637, when Cotton Mather exclaimed: "On this day we have sent six hundred heathens to hell"; the "Brown Bess" that Solomon Lombard, Thomas Lumbert's great-grandson, took as a pioneer to Gorham, Maine, in his radical rebellion against another English king (aiming this weapon at a British warship, his son fired the first shot in Maine's revolution); the flintlock musket that Consider Tiffany, my ancestor eight generations back, used in the French and Indian War in 1756, on patrol against the Indians 180 years to the month before I was wounded; the eighteenth-century Kentucky long rifle that Peter Zachary, my mother's ancestor, carried when he migrated from Virginia to Burnt Corn, Alabama, where marauding Cherokees burned the crop in 1808 or 1809; the nineteenth-century plains rifle and Colt repeating pistol of Solomon's grandsons, Stephen and James, the weapons that protected them on their migrations to Mississippi and Texas just before the Mexican-American War of 1846; the .58-caliber Minié-ball weapon of the Civil War, used by my great-great-uncle, wounded for the North, and my great-grandfather, wounded for the South; the Winchester repeating rifle that won the West in the last half of the nineteenth century, cherished by my forebears on their migration from Massachusetts to Mississippi, the weapon they used to teach my father and my uncles how to hunt.

This three-century inheritance of weapons, wars and woundings is far stronger and far deeper than we dare to think in our modern time, when computers and high technology have abolished the fact of hand-to-hand combat. This inheritance lies beneath the sophistication of our machines, linking us today, as it did for me when I was a boy, to more primitive definitions of war and masculinity and honor. This inheritance was passed from generation to generation of men by little gestures, head nods, values communicated without speaking, contests on the sporting field, all deep blood memories of what a man was supposed to be, memories of a past almost beyond conscious recall, long before there were written histories. The battles of Marathon and Salamis, *The Iliad* and *The Odyssey*, Alexander's conquests, the Peloponnesian War; the Caesars' wars, the invasions of the Goths, the Norman conquests, the Crusades for Christian honor; Agincourt, Henry V, Cromwell and the Roundheads. And, oh, the pioneers' dominance of the American landscape, wars of those ten generations of my American ancestors: Pequot, King Philip's bloody death, seventy years of conflicts between the English and the French, each side with its Indian allies. Then the Revolution (those tough Scotch-Irish who fought the English, having fled a failed revolt of their own against the king), when American victory was won through terrorism. The Sons of the American Revolution were tough sonsabitches, adept in the application of lash and tar and feather, riding the Tories out of town on a rail. All those wars when we fought for territory against red and yellow men, expelling the Cherokees into the Trail of Tears, pursuing Osceola into the Everglades, conquering the Southwest in the Mexican-American War. The bloody conflict over slavery and states' rights, our Civil War the first of modern, industrialized wars, fought by those lean and hard men, my ancestors.

When I was born, the Civil War was less than sixty years past, almost as close as World War II is to the children of today. As part of my education, Dad took me to the battlefield of Gettysburg. I could have been no more than ten or twelve as we stood at the bottom of the mile-long slope up which General Pickett led his thirteen thousand Confederate soldiers to their death from hidden Yankee fire.

Dad did not say much. Just pointed.

"We were here, boy. They were there."

What a man must do: die for his country without complaint, proudly, for his honor and his love for his nation.

My inheritance of the military tradition, begun in those years after the Civil War, was institutionalized in the nation in ways never imagined before. A direct line exists from that war through the wars against the American Indians to the Spanish-American War, both world wars, Korea, Vietnam and today's efforts in Central America and the Middle East.

That inheritance was embedded in my flesh and heart and soul by folk tales, family legends, all manner of historical accounts. As a boy, had I not known men who fought in the Civil War and then rode shotgun on stagecoaches in the West? Did not my father teach me of the long line of military honor in our nation? In the Civil War, not just Robert E. Lee and Stonewall Jackson in the South but also Generals Grant and Sherman in the North, Miles and Custer and Crook of the Indian Wars, Leonard Wood and Arthur MacArthur of the Spanish-American War, Pershing of World War I, my General Patton of 1944.

This military tradition is a direct descendent of the wars of the frontiers—not gentlemanly fights but brutal battles to the death where no quarter was given to the enemy, military or civilian. The Spanish-American War and the Philippine Insurrection that followed a civil war, where General Leonard Wood surrounded a Moro camp in 1906 and killed six hundred tribesmen, women and children; the Civil War in the summer of 1864, when Grant fought through the Wilderness, the first battle of murderous attrition; Sand Creek in Colorado, where Colonel Chivington said of Indian children, "Kill and scalp all, big and little. Nits make lice"; the Paxton Riots in Pennsylvania in the 1760s, when Scotch-Irish murdered helpless Indian captives.

This tradition culminated in the war of my father's: the fighter plane, the romantic "dogfights," the doughboy hero of World War I—even my uncle there in combat, there at Saint-Mihiel, there at the Meuse-Argonne near Verdun, where I myself entered combat in 1944 . . . This my inheritance, this my sense of manhood.

At the deepest core of that inheritance—a century of war and violence—I as a man learned that all my life I would be encircled by enemies, that reality consisted of both light and dark, the dark far more powerful than the light, as if the meaning of life itself came from the existence of my enemies. Our enemies set the boundaries as to who we were: we defined ourselves in action and reaction to our enemies on the killing grounds of war. Enemies defined our patterns of life and death. It was impossible for a man to express compassion (a "feminine" characteristic). No. The masculine creed embraced Duty, Honor, Country. Even our sleep was haunted by nightmares of dark forces that could overwhelm us and seize us and turn us into nothingness. My masculinity depended on the nature of my enemies and my need to triumph over them, my need to "stand tall" over those who threatened my nation's people and demand their unconditional surrender.

Justice Oliver Wendell Holmes, Jr., wounded three times in the Civil War, said it best: "Between two groups [of men] that want to make inconsistent kinds of worlds, I see no remedy except force." The character of the American male had been determined by participation in war and acts of violence.

Maturity, the maturity I was to have by the time I turned eighteen, the maturity of my generation—American, English, Dutch, Belgian, French, German, Russian, Spanish, Italian, Austrian, Hungarian, Czechoslovakian, Yugoslavian, Albanian, Grecian—our maturity was contained within a world of enemies, our inheritance of technological and patriotic violence, the need to be victorious, master of the killing grounds on which we fought and would, we believed, be triumphant, true to the rifles of our fathers.

CHAPTER 3

THE VOICES OF MY MOTHERS

> [After the South was defeated in the Civil War]
> *the women in every community seemed to far out-*
> *number the men; and the empty sleeve and the crutch*
> *made men who had unflinchingly faced death in battle*
> *impotent to face their future. . . . So in these days of*
> *awful uncertainties when men's hearts failed them, it*
> *was the woman who brought her greater adaptability*
> *and elasticity to control circumstances, and to lay the*
> *foundations of a new order.*
> —Caroline Merrick, *Old Times in Dixie Land*

My childhood had another world besides masculine killing grounds. The woman's tradition contained no tools of death or harsh images of enemies. It centered on her home, her friends, her church, her Bible and, most of all, her children. Her values were so different, her emotions so uniquely special that, more often than not, in the South before World War II, she created places of great purity, the only refuge in a whole society of killing grounds where men lived and died.

And even with age, as I lie in bed at night almost near sleep, I still hear the soft, gentle voices of those women: "Eddie, where are you? Eddie, watch that pot. Bring me a towel. That's a love . . . " Words warbled and cooed into my young ears. There was laughter as they sat on Grandma Green's open porch and snapped their beans, telling old tales of love and pain. There were smiles as they sewed their quilts, songs as they baked cornbread and muffins, churned their milk, broke kindling for the black iron stove, slopped the hogs, lifted cawing chickens to take the just-laid egg. All those once-heard voices merged into a sweet melody I can still hear when I listen in the silence of my heart—the same melody that warmed my grandfather, my father and my uncles when they were boys—the power of the southern woman, at the core of family life.

These women were totally dependent upon their men. They had no power, no control over their property or even over their own bodies. In the deepest sense they were economic slaves, owning nothing but themselves. Yet, from their slavery, their bodies, their sex, they made a society tolerable, created homes free of masculine violence, man's terrible need to kill.

It was their cooking: rolls and muffins, ham and chicken, rice and grits, black-eyed peas, snap beans, okra, fish rolled in corn meal and fried golden-brown in the pan, wild venison, squirrel, rabbit (best of all, wild turkey fed on acorns and wild grain, the best, lightest, most succulent meat ever cooked), and pound cakes almost pure butter, angel food cakes rich and creamy in the mouth. It was all the wonderful condiments they canned in the late summer and early fall—jams, jellies, preserved figs, fresh honey from the comb. It was the clothes they made for us, the doodads they crocheted—doilies, cozies for teapots, tablecloths, bedspreads, coasters. It was the marvelous stories they told, humor and laughter rich from their sweet lips. It was the very shape of their bodies, soft, swelling breasts never held in a brassiere, there for the child to rest against, to suckle, to hold in peace. It was the woman's world, out of the biological fact of mothering, the cultural role of housekeeping: out of slavery, power created.

It is fashionable now to deny that power, to center only on the slavery, but it was the very existence of the special world they created that made the South a safe place for children. Perhaps it was the only moment in the history of the nation—that period between the end of the Civil War and the beginning of World War II—when, for an instant, women established a world of their own, rooted in the defeat of their men. The southern male was the only American man to lose at everything: first the Civil War, then two major depressions, then populism, the radical political movement decimated in the elections of 1896. My great-grandmothers in the 1860s, my grandmothers in the l890s, my mothers in the 1920s gathered their power out of the woundings of their men.

The greatest contribution of the southern male to the culture of the South in that era of violence and killing grounds was the Ku Klux Klan. Founded in Tennessee in l866 for the sole purpose of intimidating blacks, it quickly spread throughout the South: murder, rape, arson, the repression of blacks and even white Republicans who sought a new freedom for former slaves. Lynching became the male solution to controlling rebellion, not just outright radicalism but perceived subversion. Economic prowess, accusations of rape, talking back, even suspicious looks were causes for obscene murder, eye gouging, castration, burning alive, two or three hundred recorded deaths a year. (We will never know how many occurred without public recognition.) My father was raised in Mississippi at the height of this violence, and he had a photograph of a live oak in Moss Point, where he was born, which he passed around at bridge parties when I was a child: "That's where they lynched the niggers, Eddie."

To any southern child it was obvious that the women were the strength. The men were like naughty children themselves with their drinking and their whoring, their fabrications and their promises seldom kept. But it was the women, crocheting silently in their corner, dark eyes flashing in the firelight, who always made the basic human decisions. Within those huge, extended families, women were the strength that held us all together.

Perhaps it was because the world in which I lived as a child was a primitive rural world, where each person and family depended upon their neighbor, where links of blood were the main source of survival. (Until I was five or six the only home I remember was Grandma Green's small farm in Springhill, Alabama, because in those years Dad moved us so often our houses never really settled into my consciousness.)

These women understood their power. They would not have grasped the word "role"; that was for actresses, people who played a part in life. Life was no game for them. It was a deadly matter; bad luck or a bad decision could result in the loss of all one held dear. That insecurity created courage and dignity instead of fear—and a powerful instinct to protect their children from killing grounds.

My mother's seven sisters had so many children, all near my age. We played cars in the red sandy soil under Grandma's shaded porch, using oyster shells for shovels as we dug deep in that mysterious dirt. And lying there we shared the first exploration of our souls and our bodies with each other, the sweet spring rains wetting innocent and open mouths. We explored the fields, warned by loving aunts and mothers about the deadly snakes that lay in wait for us. We walked barefoot through the chicken shit, collected eggs from the hens, watched our grandfather slaughter hogs, cutting their throats as they squealed, blood darkening the ground. We saw him swing the chickens around his head until their bodies flew from their necks.

In the summers we went to Bayou la Batre and Coden, where my father's family vacationed. We waded in the muddy flats, shot minnows with our BB guns, caught crabs on old fish line and yelled as they pinched our toes. We fished in the glaring sun, where the bobber would get lost in the flat reflection of afternoon rays, yanking in when the speck struck, body flapping on the wooden thwarts.

To the best of my memory, the world the women made for their children was one without violence, a haven from the terrible rage of the southern male. For me it became a place of enormous love and caring. My mother's roots were the King James Bible, especially the books of Matthew, Mark, Luke and John. I must have known the Sermon on the Mount before I was six or seven. I mastered the catechism before I was five.

My mother revered those words she made me learn. She struggled to order her life about them and longed for me to do the same. She made every effort to protect me from my father's overwhelming demands for conformity to the masculine ideal of conflict and violence. When he was out with friends or traveling as a salesman and cotton broker, the tension I sensed in my mother relaxed. She always seemed to be struggling to maintain her sense of balance around Dad.

From my mother I learned of justice at an early age. Much of her sense of justice came, once again, from the defeats all her men had known. Not just the losses of the war but the terrible economic failures of the 1870s, 1880s and 1890s. Those defeats coalesced into populism, the only native American radical movement that almost worked. For a moment, farmers—black and white—came together, fighting the crop lien system that took away their land.

But, again, their hopes were decimated with the defeat of William Jennings Bryan in 1896. All that remained was a memory of equity. My mother's fierce sense of justice came from that past, those failures. Her family in rural Alabama had been intimate to that struggle. From her I learned what real radicalism meant: refusal to accept any system at all, knowing that systems were, by their very nature, corrupt.

One did not "put down" others less fortunate. One did not lie or steal. One gave part of one's goods to the poor. One tithed. One never denigrated people of color. One honored one's parents and put no other images before God. My mother created decency, calmness and grace in our home, bestowing an inheritance of trust and generosity.

Yet neither she nor the other women of my family were weak or sentimental. Mothers, aunts, grandmothers, great-grandmothers joined together deep in my heart, creating a place in which I rested, secure, free from male violence. Whenever my mother caressed me just before I fell asleep, her brown eyes liquid, warm, her fingers a gentle brush over my skin, her voice gently humming her favorite song *tiptoe through the tulips with me,* whenever we played games around the dining room table (her sweet laughter encouraging me to win at Rook or Monopoly), whenever she cooked my favorite breakfast (fried bananas with hot biscuits) or my favorite dessert (icebox lemon pie), I settled into a deep security, the certainty that nothing could hurt me, joyous in my flesh and soul.

Her voice, the voices of my many mothers resonate deep within, a melody living in the caverns of my unconscious, warming and protecting me, a melody always heard when I see their photographs, the kaleidoscope of flesh and face prompting the just-remembered scent of body-warmed perfume. The melody comes too when I read their letters, hearing their honey-sweetened voices, alive again as I hold each page, mesmerized by memories.

I did not realize then, of course, the enormous price those women paid for giving me such protection, a life outside of killing grounds. Only with age have I come to understand the primitive living conditions they faced and the discipline and love required to make a home for their children and their men.

Their letters to each other have given me this understanding. When Dad died, scattered throughout his many papers were thousands of letters written by these women. Starting in the 1840s, they describe the conditions they faced each day in that pioneer world, the effort homemaking required, and, most of all, the great love they bore for their children.

The letters begin with my great-grandmother, Lydia Antoinette Tiffany, who migrated south from Connecticut after the Civil War with her husband, Oliver Wood. That migration from New England to Mississippi took twenty years. Marked by terror and poverty, it was chronicled in her letters to her mother, father, brother and her niece, Fanny Tiffany DeBrall, in Blandford, Massachusetts. These letters form the portrait of an enormously brave and compassionate human being whose strength and love made her the center of her family—and also killed her. She worked morning, noon and night as cook, maid, nurse. She made the family the source of life when they were tenant farmers, slaves to the crop lien system, when her husband was almost killed by a rattlesnake, when the family was separated by the swamps along the Mississippi River and she sent one of her sons to Arkansas to find his lost brother. She was not just a courageous woman but also the rock on which her men rested.

Her letters were sent to the family she left when she married Oliver Wood. For her, those scenes of youth, those blue-green hills of western Massachusetts, those forests of pine and hemlock and laurel, autumns of gold and scarlet, contained a memory of lost purity and innocence—far, far from southern humidity with its bugs and sickness and sweat, an image of hell. In one letter, she wrote:

> ... *I often sit and think of home and all the dear ones there I would love to see once more so much. I cannot be weaned from the scenes of my youthful days. How like a dream. I am now past 50. I can hardly realize it though I expect you would think by my looks I was 60. My hair is very grey and I wear glasses that I think Bro. Nelson wore last. He was I think 67 when he died.*

She described that primitive southern world in which she lived with great, compelling force:

[to Mr. Bela Tiffany]

> *Hamburg*
> *Ashley Co., Ark.*
> *Dec. 29th, 1878*

> *My Dear Parents & Brothers & Sisters & all:*
> ... *Geo and Wallace were away picking cotton. They picked over 7000 lbs at 50 cts per hun and board. Our crops were light last year, not making enough to pay expenses. The land was too old and poor not what it was represented to us. We had to let one horse go to get out of debt. We did not like the community we were in at all. We tried all the*

fall to make our arrangements to go back to Miss, not the Piney Woods but across the River, but everything was against us. We came down here (20 miles below Lacy) in the first place thinking the boys could earn mans hire picking cotton as the crops are generally later but the weather got so cold they did not pick but about two weeks. Oliver has finally bargained here for a place of 120 acres, 20 acres cleared. There are some young apples and peach trees. There are tolerable build-ings on the place, a well of water but it is hard. O. has got me a kerosene oil barrel for rain water.

We came here 7 weeks ago. We had to come with Mr. Finley the man we bought the place of. It made a house full. 12 in all. They moved out last Monday. He had a house to build before he could move. O. and the boys helped him. He took our double harness and wagon in part payment for the place. We are to pay $200: 4 years to pay it, the first payment is nearly paid, $50. I am in hopes now we may have something, though I cannot help but feel we have left far better places than this. But I am glad to stop anywhere. I expect its as healthy as any place in Ark. We have got along without paying a Dr's bill this year, but have taken lots of medicine to keep from being sick.

Monday Morning
January 13th, 1879

I will make an attempt to finish this letter. We are having such cold bad weather that its about all I can do to cook & keep warm and do my best. I couldn't keep warm for two months as we have had very cold weather, the worst winter thats been known for years. My dish

*water will freeze on the table before I can finish.
Our house is very cold but if we can have our
health I think we will be better fixed before
another winter. We can buy lumber at the mill
at $10 per thousand. We are 12 miles from
Hamburg. I feel as if we were almost out of the
world. There is a mill about 4 miles from us.
Our mail accommodations are bad especially
in the winter. We dont have any papers. I had
hoped we should have one of some kind this
year but money seems to be out of the question.
I tried to keep my dollar you sent to get me a
dress but we got out of coffee and I feel as if I
could not get along without it, so away it went.
Its terrible hard times. I feel sometimes as if I
couldn't stand it but I suppose the back is fitted
for its burden and I try to be thankful that I am
no worse off than I am. I think of you all very
often and am very thankful to receive letters
from F & G.*

[to Mr. Levi D. Tiffany]

*Hamburg
Ashley Co, Ark.
May 22nd, 1879*

*My dear Brother and Family,
    Your last kind letter mailed Feb. 19th was
received and ought to have been answered
before this. My time is pretty well taken up and
to tell the truth its not much of the time I feel
like writing. I feel sometimes as if there were
not many bright spots and since hearing of our
Dear Father's death, life is lonelier than ever, it
don't seem possible that he is gone, though he
has been spared long years to us. It is a great*

consolation to me that he did not suffer a long time at the last bit it came so sudden to us all. I know our old home must be very lonely now. So lonely to our mother.

. . . This is a good country to make a living in if it was only healthier, but we both regret that we came south. We would have been better off if we had stayed in Miss. for it was healthy there but I thought it was going to be better for the boys here and it would be if they could be well. I have some very kind neighbors. I always do have and am very thankful for it.

There are a great many poison snakes here. Some very large rattlesnakes, if one was to bite him [Eddie, my grandfather] he wouldn't live to get home. Oliver got bit last year close to the house. It was just at night and we had no whiskey until Geo. went to Lacey's 2 1/2 miles. I put on turpentine & soda & wet clay and everything I could think of. It pained severely and commenced swelling. I finally thought of kerosene oil. I had read of that being used in the newspaper. I applied it and it eased immediately. He took a tablespoonful inwardly when G. came we gave whiskey enough to make him drunk and sicker man you never saw. He was bit on the top of his foot. The swelling went nearly to his body. It was a long time getting well. About two weeks ago they killed a big rattlesnake that had 9 rattles and a button. Its fangs were I think 3/4 of an inch long. They are ugly looking things sure.

. . . Oh, H. if you had six men to take care of every day I am afraid you would be tired and so many inconveniences as I do, but I dont mean to complain. I feel sometimes as if my lot were a pretty hard one.

[to her mother]

Concordia,
Boliver Co., Miss.
Mar. 8, 1880

. . . The month of Jan. was very pleasant like spring and went to ploughing to break up the land. There are about 900 acres in this plantation. We are to have 30 to put 25 in cotton which will make on an average in a good season 1 bale to the acre, corn from 40 to 50 bush to the acre. If we can have health we have no fears but what will come out alright. We had to get in debt considerable to begin with coming over here. . . . We had to leave everything in the shape of furniture except my rocking chair and O's big armed chair, which we carried from Miss. to Ark. and now back again. If we can have our health here we like the country well enough. Its a good place to make money. We are about 3 miles from the river here and where we cant get anything we want with money or go where we please without crossing swamps. I dont expect to ever cross the Miss. swamps again.

[to her mother]

Concordia
Boliver Count., Miss.
Oct. 29th, 1880

. . . There has hardly been a day since somewhere near the middle of July but I have had someone sick in bed some 2 days and some three. You need not wonder that I am near worn out. Its been bilious fever and chills &

fever the worst way we ever had. Oliver is down now, had a hard chill today. His health is very poor, he can scarcely get about not done a day's work in over two months. About two weeks ago he took a terrible cold in his head and both his ears gathered and run. It made him quite ill and he dos not get over it. . . .

[to her mother]

> Cross Roads
> Jackson County, Miss.
> Aug. 13, 1883

. . . this hot weather its all I can do to do any work. Geo. says he dont see but he will have to get married to get someone to help me. Tuesday morning and all as shiftless as ever . . . seems as if I can hardly stand it through the hot weather. It lasts so long. . . . I like my new Bible so much. Ask anyone please who Davids mother was and what was the name of the daughter of the Pharoah that took Moses out of the rushes. If you find out let me know.

This was the world—violence, illness, primitive living conditions—in which my grandmothers, aunts, mothers made homes for their children and their men. I even knew one of those great-grandmothers, Grandma Watson, born in 1849, who died in 1938, the year I turned fourteen. She was Stephen Lombard's daughter. Stephen, Solomon Lombard's grandson, migrated south from Maine to work in the lumbering of longleaf pines in Mississippi in the 1840s. Grandma Watson spent the Civil War in Mobile, Alabama, and in 1864, at sixteeen years of age, divorced her first husband and married a Yankee soldier after the war. In New Orleans in the 1890s and 1900s she ran a seaman's bethel, a missionary home for poor sailors. Her bethel was only a few miles from Storyville, where jazz was born (also the largest legal whorehouse district in the United States, perhaps the world, at the time). My father spent his childhood and early youth in New Orleans at her bethel and also at his family home in Moss Point on the Gulf Coast of Mississippi.

There are voluminous letters from her daughter, Maud Watson, my father's mother, of whom Lydia once wrote to Fanny: "Eddie has married and is living with us. He married a girl from New Orleans. She is good hearted but has been petted and humored until she don't know anything else. Not a wife for a poor man. She may learn. I hope so for E's sake. . . ."

Maud's letters tell of her social life, her parties. But more: her eye for beauty, her sensitivity to light and color, form and field, her ability to experience joy in the sensuous world, the home she made for her children.

[to Fanny]

Moss Point,
Miss.
1906 (?)

> *. . . everybody in the place turned out to hear John Sharp Williams, a representative for Senator in Congress. Well, we went to Pascagoula in the electric cars, a distance of four miles, and, oh, how I wish I could paint for I'd surely send you a picture, the grand old bay, waves rippling as with a gurgle of delight and moonshine on the water, looked as if the whole expanse was a sheet of silver, with diamond reflections, then, to your back, Anderson's Park with hundreds of electric lights. . . .*

[to Fanny]

Moss Point,
Miss.
1908 (?)

> *. . . our oldest boy, Ollie, graduated from high*
> *school last week was valedictorian and won the*
> *scholarship medal. He was just sixteen last*
> *February. He is to go to college (Ol' Miss) this*
> *fall . . . I gave him a reception—color scheme,*
> *red and white (class colors). My dining room*
> *looked beautiful, had twelve red candles and*
> *red shades made of red roses. I made pictures of*
> *red and white ribbons with red roses. . . .*

At the core of all these women lay their compassion,
their love for their children, their capacity to discipline
themselves to express that love. When Lydia's daughter-in-
law died before her husband, Lydia, in spite of age and illness,
became a mother again, no matter the personal cost.

[to Cousin Fanny]

Moss Point,
Miss.
Nov. 25th, 1888

> *. . . I hardly know where to begin. I have so*
> *much care I can hardly collect my senses. Geo's*
> *wife died the 29th of October and he came*
> *home the following Saturday bringing little*
> *Cora. She is a dear little thing but a great care.*
> *She was 2 years old the 6th of October. . . .*

[to Cousin Fanny]

> *. . . I feel lonely. Geo. was married (again) the 16th of October and he has Cora. I cannot tell you how much I miss her. It almost seems as if one of the family were dead. She was a great care and responsibility still if I had felt able to care for her I could not have given her up. I was willing to keep her and the little thing wants to stay with me. . . .*

A generation later when my Grandpa Green died long before his wife, my Grandma Green was immediately forced to earn a living so as to keep her youngest child at home. Grandpa had driven a school bus until his death in 1936. Though Grandma Green had never driven in her life, the day after the funeral she marched to the bus parked in the back driveway, mounted the driver's seat as if it were a mule, and, in two days, learned to navigate safely enough to pick up, deliver, and carry home the children—to the delighted applause of her neighbors and the hearty approval of the school board. Later, so as to continue her support of that child, she bought a small apartment house, which she maintained arduously until her death in her eighties.

The love of these women for their children was so well expressed by Lydia in her many references to her son, Eddie, my grandfather:

> *. . . I wish for Eddie's sake you could have him so he could have school priveleges. He dearly loves to read and he reads very well. I am confident he would make a first class scholar. He is more interested in history than any child I ever saw. He has been reading the life of Washington & now he will put away his stories in the Companion and,*

pshaw, Washington is the best of all: I wish he could read the book you had of Wash. and his Gens. Since his father has had to give up he helps them in the field. I dont like to give him up. I claim him to help me. He went to school last summer three months, all he has ever been. There is to be a free school about 2 1/2 miles from here. I don't know whether E. will go or not, its a long way for him and hardly safe.

. . . There are plenty of wild flowers in bloom. Eddie brought me in a nice bouquet this morn. Said I could have it for the dinner table.

I had Mrs. Bette McGinnis and little boy to dinner. Had a wild turkey for dinner that E. killed last evening. He has never shot a gun but very little. He told me he was going after a Turkey. I laughed at him. I had no idea he could kill one. He took me by surprise when he came with it. He got a squirrel too.

. . . We cannot have any health here in this southern climate. Its been near 8 years since we came south. Long enough trial I think. . . . Today we are all up. O. is improving a little. Last night we had a heavy frost, water as thick as window glass. I feel so much better since it has turned cool. I have better health than anyone in the family. I have had a few chills and been right sick for a few days. I am truly thankful for it. Things go to destruction when I am laid up. Eddie is the best little fellow to help me. Getting to be a big boy and soon will be 10 years old.

. . . We are in a country where there is but little morality, no schools or churches near. A bad

place for the boys but I hope we can keep them from getting bad. Our dear little Eddie one of the best of boys its too bad on his account. He can read well. He reads Youths Companion as much as any of us.

. . . Eddie's schoolhouse closed last week. He has got along well I think. Has been through Davis Arithmetic and is now reviewing. He will be 15 the 21st of Dec. and as tall as I am. Has grown so fast this past year. . . .

My mother evinced a similar love for me; as in this letter written on the train from Chicago to Mobile, just before we moved to La Grange, Illinois, where we lived while Dad commuted to his office in the Loop:

[to my father and me]

October 1938

Dearest Ones,

You probably did not expect a train letter, did you?

As soon as it was dark, Eddie, I started wondering if you were inside. Sometimes you stay out until it is quite dark. Wish you would come in before dark while I am away. . . .

Surely hated to leave you, Eddie, and really I just wanted to get right off and stay there with you. You looked so sweet standing there throwing me kisses. I know the ladies on the train that were looking at you wished you belonged to them.

A goodnight kiss (and, Eddie, don't forget to say your prayers and drink your orange juice every a.m.),

Lots of love
Mom

These letters, these memories of my many mothers, unite in a mighty hymn in my mind's heart, a melody sung by women who survived any test and, what is more, survived it with dignity and compassion, compassion wrenched from their very bowels even when the club was at the head and the knife at the throat, even then reaching across the gap that separates us each from the other so as to caress another's soul. Yes: survived with dignity and with grace, for they lived in some other rhythm, far different from the one driving the city and the machine, a rhythm that, being timeless, embraced all time, touched earth and sweat and labor, knew that there were limits, that, without limits, there was no life. Life and death were inseparable and, thus, there was no need for fear.

The voices of my many mothers still sing to me, a promise of what life might yet be, free of my fathers' killing grounds.

PART III

MY SEARCH
FOR MEANING

CHICAGO
NEW YORK
CONNECTICUT

1943–1958

CHAPTER 4

WAR: CONFRONTING THE DILEMMAS OF MY PERSONALITY

> *He must have been young once, that General, just as all generals started from pink and slobbering babies . . . you had to suppose that the General once clasped small arms round a woman's neck; loved, hated, feared, wondered, trembled at the shadows; that once his mind threw out tendrils to grasp at the strange things that happened round him; to pull them back so that it could chew them, digest them and make something new out of them somehow. You had to try and understand the change, to find out when and why that mind—the mind of all generals, the mind of the army—shut itself against all but pre-conception and became a sausage machine, turning out uniform sausages at one end, no matter what you put in at the other.*
>
> —Robert Henriques, *No Arms, No Armour*

At birth I entered the American cauldron, conflict between my inheritance of masculinity and femininity. An impenetrable wall separated the sexes from each other.

My conflict was exacerbated by the fact that Dad, like most successful businessmen, was seldom home during the week. He traveled throughout small towns of the Deep South, honing the skills as a salesman that, one day, would make him a millionaire.

And while he sought his power on the road, my mother poured out her love upon me, held me, stroked me, nursed me, her soft breasts with their dark-brown nipples, my fierce and relentless gums sucking me deeper into her woman's world, a world she knew I must someday reject if I was to become a man, a world so far from the killing grounds where I must survive as a stranger and alone, the place a man belonged.

My mother took me into the woman's world while my father spent his nights in little towns and big cities in Louisiana, Texas, Mississippi, Alabama, Georgia, North and South Carolina—lonely nights in those small towns, great bats circling in the honey-yellow street lamps. The buzz of cicadas pressed deep into night's purple darkness, heat dripped sweat over the loins. Dad learned his trade in those small towns and their stores, selling paint by the boxcar, shrewdly honing his skills, learning how to recognize those he must influence, how to read another's greed and use it for himself. Using his marvelous intuition, he could sell anything to anyone. He began to accumulate his first fortune out of the bleeding, broken, poverty-stricken South. He would never be poor again!

Ah, but the nights, the lonely nights on the road, away from his family and their support. His lonely presence in hotel rooms and in bars, the sterile conviviality, brought in the money that would make him rich so he could give his family the goods that his parents, the whole South, had lost in the Civil War. But what really belonged to him in those towns? What could he call his? Where could he soothe his loneliness? Where else but with the whore, the hooker? A moment's explosion followed by the swift slide into guilt and depression.

Oh, this my father's world, the killing grounds of business in the 1920s in which he lived and prospered. His wife now more mother than lover, turning her passion to her son (who one day must reject her to become a man). His life alone four or five nights a week in barren hotel rooms in that land of cane and honey, seizing the hooker, the whore, the Ladies of Storyville, the ladies of his youth in New Orleans, of his years in the Air Service of World War I. These the dictates of his tradition of masculinity, the inheritance he passed to me, the rifles of his fathers, used to fuel his demand for power and unparalleled material wealth in the barren wastes of America.

Be a man, my son!

To become a man, to imitate my father, to be a master of killing grounds, required repression of all those qualities of my mothers, as though being a woman, a person with a vagina and all its secretions, with breasts and their flowing milk, was the greatest of human sins: the color and taste and smell of a woman's fluids would stain my image, wash away my masculinity. I must repress and squash, squeeze and maim those qualities within myself: kill the sparrow and the rabbit, shoot the gulls and the pheasants, slay my enemy on the field of battle.

They were there, boy. We were here.

Like to be soft, boy? Gentle? A goddamn woman? DO HOUSEWORK WITH YO' MOMMA? Are you a MAN, boy? CAN YOU GET IT UP EVERY TIME? CAN'T GET IT UP IF YOU'RE A SISSY, BOY.

BE HARD, BOY!

A ROCK. A man.

My mothers were, by far, the better persons.

But . . . be a MAN, my son.

The conflict intensified as I reached puberty and learned of girls and sex. Stick my hard thing up a girl's crack? Do that to a woman like my momma? Make love to the place I came from?

It sickened me. Yet the folklore I learned in high school told me that it must be done if I was to enter manhood.

> *There once was an Indian maid*
> *Who never was afraid*
> *To lie on her back*
> *In the middle of a shack*

64

And let some cowboy
Shove it up her crack.

Oh, how she was surprised
When her belly began to rise
And out popped a nigger
With a cast iron trigger
And an asshole 'twixt his eyes.

We looked for women as if we were beasts of prey. We went to taxi dance halls where for a dime we danced for three minutes, the first time I ever felt the soft wonder of a woman's breast. Some of my friends were more adventurous and sneaked into whorehouses, where they got laid on Saturday night for two dollars. All of us necked in the back seat of our father's car, tongue to tongue, thigh to thigh, trembling on the verge of orgasm.

All socialization of our sexuality was centered on denying our softness and gentility. Women were fair game, a man's goal was to force her on her back, hold her down, squeeze her, stick it in her, that most terrible of American masculine juvenile daydreams: a woman tipped up, helpless beneath a man, while he forced her, took her, tore at her, fingers and lips and fists, hearing her pleas for more.

To become a man, we denied all our compassion and softness. The worst accusation? "Ol' Ed? Hell, Ed ain't no man. He's a goddamn woman. A fuckin' queer." We would do anything to prevent those words.

Anything.

The hardest test for me came on the football field. At eight or nine years I started to play. Though I never told anyone, the game terrified me. On Friday nights before a game I could not sleep. I would get up in the dark and turn on the water in the washbowl so Dad would not hear me puke. I did not want him to hear the evidence of my fear.

For I played. I went to the field and fought and sweated and yelled and screamed and took out my fear and terror on other boys, smaller than I, whenever I could find them, knowing that Dad stood on the sidelines, his fat cigar rolling between his lips.

To be a man was to be hard, play football, win, score, treat women as a "piece of ass," hold her as prisoner, do with her as you liked, twist those breasts, stick something hard up her crack, yes, by GOD! Deny the juices in yourself. There are enemies out there, boy, to get you if you go soft . . . you'll get carved up if you aren't hard as a rock on the killing grounds of life.

Dominate. Control. Master. Defeat your enemies.

O ut of those conflicting worlds of masculinity and femininity, out of century-old traditions, out of such ancient values, I volunteered for the infantry in World War II. From my father I had learned of killing grounds, that I must prove my masculinity by facing the "enemy" in mortal combat, vanquishing him on his territory. The values of my mother— compassion and caring, peace and justice—had to be suppressed as I became a man.

Yet never, never, never did I hear my mother, my aunts, my grandmothers oppose the war, my entry into it. Their sense of caring for those less fortunate than themselves, their faith in Christ's mercy and forgiveness, did not extend to those who had struck at their fair country. Maybe in the deepest way all my female relatives resembled the peasant women who had scourged *la femme scalpée*, approving as the Frenchman cropped her hair? Maybe, when a woman's world was finally threatened by a killing ground, anger there, but always repressed, must explode? Maybe her hatred in war was the greatest hatred of all? Hatred for the enemy from the woman threatened by him? Even more hatred for his wife or mistress, whore or lover, the woman who lay on her back and let the enemy's big hard prick slide easily into her vagina, who pulsed and moaned beneath his thrusts, her pleasure taken from his flesh . . . Maybe that was why the French turned on that woman the moment they were freed: scalp her who had loved the enemy of their men, scalp her who had loved it, yeah, loved it, strutting around the plaza of that small town, her hand on her big German's arm as all her former lovers raged.

When women approved of stripping another woman and cutting off her hair, when women approved of killing grounds, violence must be approved. When my mother accepted my enlistment, war must be for a good cause.

Did not my Grandma Wood support my volunteering for the draft with a letter?

> *Dallas, Texas*
> *April 3, 1943*
>
> *My Darling Eddie,*
> *Simply to say I am indeed proud of my grandson for volunteering and not being drafted. . . . You are too young but God will take care of you, for a fairer son I never knew and you have been reared properly. . . . Remember you come from a long line of soldiers, thus do right and win!*

If women supported the killing grounds of war, then it was not only proper, it was expected, it was correct for me to unite my mother's and my father's values and my mother's compassion by enlisting in the Army, glorifying those ten generations of my male ancestors and their weapons, each generation of murderous technology becoming more sophisticated, culminating at last in World War II, the greatest explosion of military weapons in the long history of the world.

War was in the air, a subtle miasma that one breathed from birth: war, a romantic event, essential to one's manhood, war the common link to all children of my generation, no matter where they lived in the Western world. All our fathers had fought in World War I. Though we rebelled against war in the early 1930s with our Oxford Pledges and our marches for peace, by the time of the Spanish Civil War in 1936, the youth of the world had acquired a faith in war as a way of life.

American, British, European, Russian, we erected a common sense of values by which to live in time of war:

A dream: *a bright illusion from my populist forebears that out of violence we could create a society of splendid peace and justice . . .*

A love of our land: *the bay spread out from the gumbo-muddy shore in soft green surges and schools of specks sped in choreographed unison through the clear salt water, seizing the minnows swirling from the diving gulls as buckets of shrimp were hauled in careless splendor to the deck of our boat, boiled in great washtubs, washed down with bottles of home-brewed beer . . .*

A family, our flesh: *the ancient brooding flesh from which I came, those great gatherings on humid Sunday afternoons beneath the moss-laden live oaks when mothers, grandmothers, aunts, uncles, kissing cousins and cousins once removed descended from the eroded fields and red-gullied farms upstate, bringing memories of days when Ol' Jack rode through the valley and Marse Robert swung up the heights of Gettysburg, frosted glasses of champagne drunk with slippery sea-salted oysters, red-gravied hickory-smoked hams and cornbread, biscuits, molasses, jams, freezers of homemade ice cream cranked with loving sweat . . .*

In these values we found our chalice and our Holy Grail. In these values we found our faith and our purity, our honor with which we would vanquish our enemy on the killing grounds of war. We were born into a century of war, the greatest the world has ever known.

L ike all other children of the world, I remained a total innocent. I had no more concept of the reality I soon would face than the just-born baby does of life. My mind swirled with images of my manhood bestriding the world. I saw myself as an officer and a gentleman, leading troops into battle, taking chances no one else dared. I was Humphrey Bogart in *Casablanca*; that was my movie, it expressed the values of a Hemingway. A man lived and died for justice on the killing grounds of the world . . . always, always, a beautiful woman waiting with glistening eyes and gentle hands, ready to comfort, cherish and support her man as he fought for a just cause.

With pure motivations and a clear mind, I volunteered for the draft in March 1943, twenty-five years to the week after Dad enlisted in the Air Service in World War I.

> *March 18, 1943*
>
> *Dear Mom and Dad,*
>
> *I have perhaps the hardest thing to tell you I have ever had to tell anyone in my life. You both know how I feel about the Army and how much I want to go in. Well, yesterday I volunteered. I know that you will hate me for doing this, but the way I look at it, it is the only honorable and decent thing to do. . . .*

That decision led me to basic training in Camp Callan, California. Then, along with all my peers who had been in college before the war, I was sent to the Army Specialized Training Program, where I studied college-level engineering while Sicily was invaded, then Italy, with preparations under way for D-day in France. I loathed being in school while others fought—yet I worked so hard I always received commendations.

Then, by the oddest quirk of circumstances, really part of Army madness, I was given the opportunity for advanced training in premedical school at the University of California at Los Angeles. I had taken an Army aptitude test and, out of thousands, scored as one of the highest in my ability to become a doctor. I was transferred out just as the engineering schools were closed to supply replacements for the invasion of France.

I was in Fatsville. School for the duration of the war. Ten thousand women and a hundred men. Yet my high school buddies were beginning to die. At basic training in Camp Callan all of us had seen a remarkable series of training movies, *Why We Fight*, teaching us about Nazi rage and Japanese treachery. The values of my generation were threatened by the enemy, symbolized, to me, by the book burnings in Germany, by Hermann Goering, fat and evil, pulling his pistol from his holster as he cried: "Whenever I hear the word 'democracy,' I take out this!"

Men died to protect my country while I studied.

> UCLA
> March 15, 1944
>
> *Dear Mom and Dad,*
>
> *. . . March is the crucial month of my life. Remember a year ago when I volunteered? Everything has turned out OK from that, hasn't it? I'd have been on a banana boat if I had waited 'till June. I guess you can figure out pretty well what is coming from this. Gosh, but I hate to tell you what I've made up my mind to do, but here goes.*
>
> *I know how much you have counted on me staying in school and going on to be a doctor, but I guess it just isn't going to pan out that way. I've discovered in the past six weeks it isn't for me. Pop, you know how it is when you dislike something intensely. You just can't study it. I don't believe that I could ever make a good doctor. And I don't want to be one unless I'm good. So I've decided to quit.*
>
> *That's about the whole deal. I could pass. I am positive. By really studying I could get to med school but I would hate it. There's another angle too—I feel pretty silly here spending the government's money and not getting a thing out of it. I guess I'm just fool enough to see it that way.*

Mother, you've instilled the principles of living up to your true self so well that I've got to believe in what I'm doing before I do it. And thank you for it! No matter where I go I will always be thinking of you and Dad and remembering all those swell trips we've had together. And looking forward to those of the future. You've been so darned good to me I can't express my thanks.

All other [engineering] schools on the coast closed yesterday. They [student soldiers] are going back. I guess that's another reason I can't see myself in school when a lot of other boys are really doing something. . . . I imagine that it will be three or four weeks before I leave. I might even finish this term—but don't count on it. I shall keep you well posted.

Mom and Dad, don't take this too hard and don't worry about me. I'll be all right!!! Because I know that deep down you agree with me. You've got to live up to your own self—or what have you—if you're going to be happy. . . . I know there will be hard times, but I hope that I can keep seeing it's the right thing. . . . Anyway, don't worry about me, and I'll write darned soon.

Your son,
Eddie

When I told the officers in charge of my unit of my decision, they thought I was crazy. The lieutenant, a little older than I, struggled to talk me out of it. The captain finally grunted and grinned: "If he wants to get killed, let him. I won't stop him." He gave me a three-day pass before shipping me out.

I picked up a woman . . . noooo, she picked me up, at the USO center in Hollywood. We talked about the war. French kissed, perhaps the second time in my life. She would not let me in her apartment; I believe now that she lived there with a man. But she gave me a book, *Mud on the Stars*, by William Huie, a fine novel about the South of the thirties, a book I still possess.

They cut my papers while I was on pass. The day after returning I was on the troop train to Oregon and a new post, Camp Hood. Four months later I was on a troop ship to France, beginning my journey into the land of the wounded.

An indelible memory I carried with me overseas was my father's last present. On my leave in June, just before I left for Europe, he took me on a canoe trip deep into Quetico National Forest just north of Ely, Minnesota, where we had fished together when I was a boy, a place that brought out the most vivid manifestation of my father's love of nature. A magic time. Only he and I, the wind, the water, the sky, a tent—and a two- or three-pound smallmouth bass at almost every cast. The wilderness before society corrupted it.

Those memories, those values, I took with me into combat as I joined the children of the world in the war that continued the one of 1914, the war to end all wars. The voices of my many mothers muted now as I shipped overseas in August 1944, carrying my M-1 rifle in my hand, a hunting knife jammed carelessly into my leggings, pursuing the image of my masculinity and the inheritance of my fathers on the killing grounds of Europe—a just war resolving the dilemmas of my personality.

CHAPTER 5

BETRAYAL

> *And that is just why they* [our fathers] *let us down so badly.*
>
> *For us lads of eighteen they ought to have been mediators and guides to the world of maturity, the world of work, of duty, of culture, of progress—to the future. We often made fun of them and played jokes on them, but in our hearts we trusted them. The idea of authority which they represented, was associated in our minds with a greater insight and a manlier wisdom. But the first death we saw shattered this belief. We had to recognize that our generation was more to be trusted than theirs. . . . The first bombardment showed us our mistake, and under it the world as they had taught it to us broke in pieces.*
>
> —Erich Maria Remarque
> *All Quiet on the Western Front*

My wounds received on the killing grounds of France irrevocably changed my life. With fierce and unrelenting energy, I pursued unexpected ways, always seeking to understand the reasons for killing and wounding, as if deep within me I listened to a whispered lament unheard by any but myself, the long wail of the sixty million killed in that war: *WHY ME? WHY ME? WHY DID*

YOU LET ME DIE IN BELGIUM, LONDON, PARIS, DUNKIRK, LENINGRAD, PEARL HARBOR, THE PHIL-IPPINES, NORTH AFRICA, OMAHA BEACH, ST. LO, STALINGRAD, DRESDEN? WHY DID YOU ALLOW THESE PLACES OF THE WORLD TO BE DESTROYED? WHY DO I LIE ALONE IN SOIL I NEVER KNEW? With this cry go faces, faces I remember of boys my age, those I knew as a child in the South or with whom I graduated from high school: Byron Hedin, killed as an air cadet in a plane crash in the fall of 1943; Bob Overmeir, splattered in Germany in 1945; Glen Davis, with whom I played as a boy in Charlotte, wounded just after me in France and to die of his wounds a week later. And the Russian refugee I sat next to in a French aerodrome while waiting for the flight to England in a Red Cross plane; I watched his bandages slowly redden with unstoppable hemorrhage as he smoked my Lucky Strikes, maybe the best gift I ever gave anyone in my life. And the paratrooper in the hospital bed next to mine in England who died thrashing, yanking the tubes from his arm as he cried for more ammunition. Faces of the dead I see as I walk the streets, sensing for an instant those ghostly, fervid features of my past, mixed and mingled among the faces of fat young college students, sleek with their dry-blown hair, faces of the dead scream to me their eternal question to us the living: WHY? WHY? WHY ME? Faces of the future as well: my children, my children's children, burned, scarred, puffy, ashed by atomic war. WHY? WHY? WHY ME? The question I have asked for these forty years, searching for the causes of wars and woundings, the inheritance of violence that led me and all the men and women of my world and time to participate in acts of unspeakable barbarity. WHY? My own life the laboratory for my exploration.

All I ever remembered immediately after the wounding, lying helpless in field hospitals in France, was the sweet, sickening smell of blood—mine, those about me in the ward.

Two or three operations shaped the torn flesh on my buttock into a great and gaping hole ten inches wide, eight inches across, four inches deep, a hole into which the doctors poured yellow penicillin each day. Another operation removed broken fragments of skull and pieces of shrapnel from my brain, leaving me still paralyzed on my right side.

My wounds healed quickly when I left those hospitals for permanent installations in England, flown over by the Medical Corps within a week. The first night in the ward, with real electric lights, I could not sleep; it had been so many weeks since I had felt real sheets, they burned my dried skin. Within days, another operation cured the paralysis of my body. The surgeon removed more shattered pieces of my skull from my brain. He worked without anesthesia, the orderly with me under the sheet talking to me throughout, insuring that the surgeon did not slip and penetrate other parts of my brain and thereby do even greater damage to my nervous system. The surgeon drilled into my skull around the wound the shrapnel had made. The vibration made me feel like I was lying on a railroad track with the engine driving over my head. The surgeon spoke to me: "You've got a brisk hemorrhage now." That was the only pain I ever felt from the head wound.

But my other wounds seemed to require a symphony of pain to complete their healing.

A piece of shrapnel lay near my bladder. The doctor inserted up my flaccid penis a catheter with a small mirror on its end, so he could search for injury. It was torture. I wanted to cry, and think I probably did. Later, I was given the wrong blood type in transfusion after one of my operations. Within minutes I was tossing wildly about on the bed as my fever rocketed.

The operation on my buttock was far more dreadful than anything else. The surgeons drew that great hole together (it had been an oddity in the ward, patients gathering around each day to stare with fascination at its red and bloody depths) using enormous stitches and clamps; it felt as if they had drawn my entire leg, its muscles, tendons and nerves up into my buttock. God! how it throbbed and jerked and trembled with pain.

Slightly nauseated, I woke up on morphine the morning after the operation, floating on a sea-tossed cloud above my bed. With each dose of morphine the nausea increased, as did the sense of distance from reality. I loathed the feeling. After days of ferocious struggle with nurses and doctors, I went off the drug, preferring pain to the disorienting sensation created by the medicine.

At the end of two months I walked again, first on crutches, then with a cane. I hobbled around the ward, waving the cane joyously, happy once more to be able to walk, to talk, to laugh.

The hole in my skull was now covered by my hair, which had grown out after being shaved bald for so long; the scars on my buttock were hidden by my clothes; the shrapnel thought to be in my belly had encysted in my hipbone.

To the world I looked normal.

The scars on my emotions were far more complicated. The healing had barely begun in those three months in France and England, where, in the ward, my psyche had been protected from all external pressures but the slow chords of recovery. There were no visitors; there were few letters; there were no flowers. Thirty or forty of us, all who had known combat in France, Holland, or Belgium, were protected and cared for, loving each other with the same tenderness I had known just behind the front. Nurses and doctors gave us special attention, serving our smallest need. Red Cross ladies came by each day with cigarettes and fruit, books and games to entertain us. They wrote my letters while I was paralyzed, brought the memory of my mothers into the ward.

Though somewhere in my deepest self I still wondered about my combat experience—wounded in the butt and only a day at the front—it did not seem very important, surrounded by men in their teens or early twenties who had their own stories to tell. I listened, heard in their voices the same relief I felt: we had survived. Even our pain told us each day that we lived, and as our flesh healed, we appreciated with increasing intensity the proof of glorious life about us, the marvelous colors of the English autumn outside our window, the rich bronze of beech trees, the caress of wind on our flesh when we were moved from ward to ward in wheelchairs or stretchers. Even the most common sensations proved we lived: the touch of sheets on our bodies, the pungent taste of cigarette smoke, the warmth from the potbellied stove that heated the ward as we sat around it smoking, drinking tea, laughing, telling stories.

I spent most of my time reading, seldom interrupted by officialdom except for four shots of penicillin each day, occasional visits from the doctor and one from an officer who pinned my Purple Heart on my chest. That time of silence, of being left totally alone, proved absolutely essential to my recovery. The books I read, the questions I asked, began my lifelong search for a life outside of killing grounds—and led to the best day I spent in England before being shipped home.

Sometime in early November 1944, I was well enough to receive a one-day pass into Salisbury, a town not far from the hospital. I had no knowledge of the town's immense and ancient cathedral, no understanding of the medieval age and the Gothic cathedrals scattered over England, France and Germany, except for the cathedral at Reims, the one my division had liberated.

The cathedral loomed above Salisbury Plain, humbling me as I approached it. Even from the distance it comforted. Inside its great spaces rising toward the heavens, inside its pearled light shimmering translucently, I suddenly knew the first peace I had experienced since my canoe trip with Dad in June, before being shipped overseas. I touched the compassion of my mother, forcefully suppressed in this war. I sank into a pew and cried like a baby, suddenly knowing that, in truth, I was safe again. A great warmth encircled me, contained me, held me, arms of my mothers, perhaps the mother of us all.

I do not know how long I cried, but when I stopped, the pain repressed since being wounded had been purged, my emotions as pure again as those of a young child. My thoughts were fresh, charged with the desire to return home, start school, read, study, struggle to change the world so that what had happened to me would never, never, oh never, happen to a young man again. I yearned to free the world of killing grounds, of the desires and emotions that had formed me.

Three months after I was wounded, I landed in New York. Though able to hobble around on a cane, officially I remained a stretcher case. I had come home on my twentieth birthday, December 12, 1944. Come home with enormous hope and sharp delight, symbolized by the way I entered the States. Strapped into a stretcher, I lay on my back below a hatch, staring up at the late afternoon sky. Above me a great crane swayed back and forth, lowering a halter through the hatch.

"Take it easy, kid," the medic murmured to me. "Ya gonna get a ride. We got so many stretcher cases to unload off this bucket, we're only taking half of 'em to shore by hand. The rest get to ride the crane. Don't worry. You'll be safe. We do this every day."

He fastened the halter to the stretcher. The crane lifted.

For a moment the stretcher twisted crazily, spun me round and round in the air. Then it steadied, lifting me slowly up and up and up, through the hatch, above the deck, straight toward the evening star.

New York's skyline spread before me under the pale blue of an autumn twilight turning pink. The Chrysler Building with its bronzed cap and spire glimmered in the falling sun, a golden flash like the wave of a welcoming hand. Beneath it the city flickered and glowed, a million beacons lighting my way home.

Home!

I had made it. I was truly alive.

Joy filled my heart. I wept as they lowered me to the ground.

But the tears I cried when I reached La Grange, returning to my parents, were no longer those of delight. Four days after I arrived home, the Battle of the Bulge erupted; my division— the guys I had known in France—was trapped in Belgium and Luxembourg by the Germans. While they were dying I had come home to my mother and father on leave; had come home to a father suddenly a wealthy man, steaks in Deepfreezes in the basement, spare tires for the car, dozens of shirts and socks, all kinds of canned goods, the fine food we had eaten before the war profligate upon the table, new suits and new shoes and new ties, all as it was in those summers we spent in Canada or on the Gulf before the war. Only now it bothered me. Where was the dream for which we had fought? FOR THESE GOODS? THESE THINGS? FOR THESE THINGS MY FRIENDS WERE KILLED? WHERE WERE PEACE AND JUSTICE, CARING AND COMPASSION? THEY BLEW ME UP IN FRANCE FOR THIS? FOR THIS I ALMOST DIED?

Against the memory of the time we liberated that French village full of slave labor workers, when we saw the joy on the faces of those freed, my wound and wounding had made sense. But here? Our neighbors complained about the blacks riding the streetcars and getting paid too much to work as servants; "uppity niggers" they were, what was the land coming to?

THEY BLEW ME UP FOR THIS?

To have my father brag about me in his club?

To have a relative ask me with great curiosity if I had killed anybody?

To know at the bottom, at the terrible depths of my soul, so fearful I could not bear to bring it to my consciousness, that all Dad's new wealth had been made from the war, from selling cotton goods to mills which then produced clothes the government bought at high prices; hating him, then, hating him suddenly and completely, hating him totally, not even seeking to understand his guilt, only filled with hate and rage, hating this man I once had loved so much, now my enemy.

My wounding made no sense.

The ideals for which I had volunteered—the dream that out of the war would come a world devoted to justice, the Four Freedoms of Roosevelt and Churchill (freedom of speech and expression, freedom of worship, freedom from want and freedom from fear)—were never mentioned, as if they had not existed.

For these material things, instead, I had damn near been killed. Was the pain I had known, these scars, a joke played upon me?

Those who called World War II a good war did not experience the one in which I fought. Most of all, they did not know what it was to come back to the United States from the land of the wounded. Even now, forty years later, I shake with the same fierce and unforgotten fury, remembering what it was to return from overseas. To suddenly see for the first time the gluttony of my homeland—its big cars, its steaks and sweet desserts, its clothes, its wine and whiskey, its parties. To understand that this is what we died for, the opportunity to make a buck. The Battle of the Bulge. Chosin Reservoir. Tet. It must have been the same for each of us warriors. We were like Roman legionnaires returning from the provinces to our triumph of gall.

The deeper I journeyed into the land of the wounded, the more alienated from my nation I became. I had left my companions behind in military hospitals and on hospital ships. The language we had spoken there and at the front had no interpreter in this place populated by civilians and strangers in what, once, had been my native land.

In January 1945 I was discharged with a medical disability, my appearance absolutely normal to any observer. The winter, spring and summer in that suburban community of La Grange were times of momentous chaos and confusion. I no longer knew who I was. I clearly was not the boy who had left; I certainly was not the man my parents wished me to be; I could no longer relate easily to my peers.

There was one solution: drink and party.

My God! I remember in awe the drunken brawls, night after night after night until two or three or four in the morning as someone else came home from Europe or back on leave from the South Pacific. Each of us told our tales of combat and war; each of us vaunted our manhood. We drank beer and bourbon and some god-awful drink that was sweet and pink, and the bed roared around our ears when we slumped into it, to rise in the morning at eleven and twelve and go to the local drugstore and raise some more hell, maybe go down to the striptease joints on Chicago's West Madison or, at least, go hear some good jazz: Muggsy Spanier or Sidney Bechet at the Blue Note. Then, later, necking in the back seat of our parents' car—hardly making love, I didn't know what it meant, but necking—everything but final penetration, coming in our underwear, our hands, her mouth. Hell, we had won the war, hadn't we?

Beneath it all was a fear so buried in my subconscious mind I could never admit it, did not know of its existence: I was terrified of women. I dared not take off my pants, expose that great red scar, evidence of what I began to fear was cowardice, to another human being. In my deepest soul I had been emasculated without understanding that terrible fact. Oh, everything worked. My penis hardened, spurted in wet dreams or masturbation. But show myself to a woman? Discuss that one day in combat? Christ!

I began to joke about it, called myself the only man in the world with a hole in his head and half an ass. I drank harder, potent in the flesh, broken in the emotions.

I grew smaller and smaller around Dad. His charisma, his force overwhelmed me, perhaps as all fathers do to young men seeking their own strength. But this was all the more exacerbated now by my wound, my growing anxiety over the specter of impotence, my rage at my father for making so much money out of the war. This man I had loved so much, this man who had walked this earth as my God—a war profiteer!

82

We were both trapped in angers not of our sweet making.

And my mother was no help at all.

In ways she did not understand, she massaged my hostility for my father. Contemptuous of his drinking, she belittled Dad in front of me, even hinting with barely repressed tears that he "played around." It was almost as if she, in her great beauty and maternity, sought in me what she could no longer find in my father.

Wounded, bitter, infuriated, I was unable to find any understanding inside myself, unable to discover it in a woman's flesh. So I found it in my mother. She made a cave for me with her strong arms, and I crept deep within it. I let her caress my pain, her maternal love becoming my source, my strength, holding back the night and its harsh terrors, the memory of my fear. She took me deep within her emotions, deep, deep, deep, her maternal desire and need so strong that she let me rest myself within her, seeking to cure my pain. Reluctantly at first, then willingly, we built a world together, a cocoon of love in which, for a time, there were only the two of us.

Oh, how we must have hurt Dad.

Did he return to his whores, his hookers, the Ladies of Storyville?

I do not know.

I only remember, immediately after the war, the heavy scent of my mother's perfume, the lovely pearl of her flesh, my mother, my mother, my mother: the only woman with whom I could relate. I was locked deep inside myself by my wound, raging inside, not even knowing it, needing the love of a woman my age, unable to reach outside myself for it, sinking deeper and deeper into her maternity, into the pain of my wound. My father now my dark enemy.

During the winter, spring and summer of 1945, in that bedroom which had been mine for years, I first began to write about my pain. Short stories about combat, a play, but most of all journals. And in them I embarked on the terrible, desperate search for a meaning to my wounding, a search for a world without killing grounds. I longed for a just society out of my wounding as if only a world dedicated to the Four Freedoms for which I had fought would make sense of my pain. If a good society came from my wounding, then it held dignity and honor. If not . . . ?

I struggled for understanding in my journals:

> *I feel I am going mad. I have no one to talk to. As if nobody understands. All the guys I buddied with in high school are overseas getting killed. Wounded. Christ! Shot at . . . and it's just the same here as it was before the war. Parties. Country clubs. . . . I want to drive a tank down the goddamn street and smash everything I see. . . . If I couldn't shut the door to this room, read, write in this journal, I would go crazy . . .*

> *I returned from overseas four months ago. I came back with ideals, a hatred for war, greed, intolerance in all its forms, complacency, all those things I thought had been abolished from my country by the war. . . . I have been a man from Mars. . . .*

> *. . . There is something enormously wrong with the world when a favored few are clean, well-fed, possess all material advantages while the vast majority of the world's population are filthy, starving, freezing, dying animals. . . . We must revert from this ever increasing tendency toward materialism. I dread to think of the condition of the world in a few generations if we do not seek other paths . . . a retrogression into another dark age.*

I twisted and turned, searching for meaning. I could not find it in that small suburb of white, middle-class Americans, as kind to me as they could possibly be, gentle, loving. My war and my wounding had given me another vision of reality.

I longed for a just society that would make sense of the violence I had experienced. My search was for an alternative to killing grounds as a way of life. And I found many of these, for a time, at the University of Chicago. I wrote in my journal that winter:

> *. . . all I know about the University of Chicago is that it has the reputation of being the most liberal and progressive university in the nation. That is all I desire—a school where studies come first, an honest attempt to make the student think, the poppycock of fraternities and sororities and football subordinated to more important things.*

I discovered at the university that I was not the only citizen in the land of the wounded. The high school classes of 1941, 1942 and 1943 had made a major contribution to the casualty lists of World War II. Beginning in the spring of 1945, I discovered many of those other pilgrims, all inducted into the land of the wounded in New Guinea or Anzio, Sicily or D-day, up the boot of Italy, all struggling with the consequences of that war, attracted to one of the few places in the nation that sought then, on the deepest level, for answers to life. The university attempted to discover solutions to killing grounds by using the intellect. Robert Maynard Hutchins, its president, believed that men and women could use their minds to free themselves from the prejudices of their past. A true education gave men and women freedom. That education consisted of a grounding in the classics, not in tools and technologies but in the great books that laid the foundation and set the frame for Western civilization.

I made friends there who shared my journey: Bill Montgomery, who went in on D-day with the Fourth Division as a stretcher bearer, hearing bullets ricochet off the steel ramp protecting him just before it dropped, so he could plunge into the surf and run toward the beach; Bob Reed, who had his arm blown off below the elbow in the Philippines; John Day, who fought through battles in Africa, Sicily and Italy as an infantryman without ever receiving a scratch; Don Mulligan, who invaded Germany with the Twentieth Armored Division; Burt Wax, who had both knees destroyed when he fell from a mountain face while training with the Tenth Mountain Division in Colorado; Paul Berger, who helped liberate the death camps in the spring of 1945 as an infantryman.

We loved each other; we could talk to each other of memories only we shared. Even with them, though, I still could not bear to reveal my inward struggle over my wound, only a day in combat, wounded in the brain, the butt, my growing fear that I had been a coward, shown the "white feather." I tried so hard to understand, while I lived in constant fear of ridicule.

Sometimes my head ached with a fierceness I could not tolerate. I went to the university hospital clinic, then to the Veterans Administration hospital. There was absolutely nothing to be done. They raised my compensation for a few months; then, when I stopped complaining, they lowered my payments again. I learned to live with those sudden pulsations in my skull: they always subsided in a few minutes, like an ice-cream headache. My right hand was still numb; little of the feeling ever returned to my fingers, but the hell with that too. After all, I *had* a hand; Bob Reed didn't.

I was still terrified of women. Oh, I went out, even was enormously attracted to one stunningly beautiful young woman. Yet, deep in my heart, I was so afraid.

But at the university I had my friends. There I searched for justice and spoke out for real changes rising from the war. I spoke at the Victory in Europe celebration at Rockefeller Chapel and, later that May, gave another speech, on the same platform with Paul Robeson, the black actor, singer and activist, later destroyed in the anti-Communist witch hunts.

I still have the speech I made, and read it now with sadness. We so longed to make a world without war:

> *One of the most oft-repeated maxims of history is that youth has paid the mistakes of age. Millions of my buddies, American and Allied, and other millions who by accident of birth were citizens of countries with which we fought, have borne the greatest burden created by the blundering stupidity and blind selfishness of our elder statesmen. These men, who have the blood of youth upon their hands, must have the idealism of youth stamped upon their consciences. . . .*

For we believed then—oh, sweet God, the marvelous naïveté of it!—we believed that men and women banded together could make a difference in the condition of the world. We returned from war, hot for change, hot for power to make a brave new world.

We struggled to create a new veterans organization, one not for privilege but for justice to all, the American Veterans Committee (AVC). We believed that we were citizens first, veterans second. We wanted a just society and not handouts as a special class.

For me and for a whole generation of my peers, AVC symbolized opportunities for a just society. It called for a program of full employment, fair housing, the embodiment of the Four Freedoms for which I had joined the Army. I quickly became an officer in the chapter at the University of Chicago. Forty-five and forty-six were exciting and wonderful years. We had won the war. And we wanted peace and justice out of that victory. But in the late spring of 1947 it all fell apart.

In 1945 my former leader, General Patton, had said we had fought the wrong army. In early 1946 Churchill had made his "Iron Curtain" speech in Fulton, Missouri. In the spring of 1947 President Truman instituted a "loyalty oath" for those who worked for the federal government. That summer the House Un-American Activities Committee investigated the Hollywood Ten.

We who had fought the war against the Nazis, we who were still so terribly young, were now told that the Russians, our former allies, who had been killed and wounded by Germans, along with us, were now our enemies. (Just as their young men were told that we were theirs.)

As an officer of the American Veterans Committee, that was exactly what I was expected to believe. The issue posed to us was simple: Communists were totalitarian, weren't they? Out to repress freedom? Would destroy our freedom if they had power? So get 'em first. Kick 'em out of liberal organizations like AVC, the same argument President Woodrow Wilson and Attorney General A. Mitchell Palmer had made in 1919 when they rounded up the Reds and sent them back to Russia.

I was so confused. How could those we had supported in the war suddenly, overnight, become our enemies? I didn't like the Communists. Hell, I KNEW they had done terrible things. Stalin's acts were as evil as Hitler's. But treating them as they would treat us stuck in my craw. What gave us the right to repress them? Why were we so arrogant, so goddamn sure of ourselves?

Which is what the fifties were all about, forgotten in our current nostalgia for that decade. Squeeze out the unpopular viewpoint. Put those who stood for their right of free speech in the slammer. Oh, we never were as bad as the Reds. We didn't physically torture anybody. WE ONLY TOOK AWAY THEIR JOBS AND DESTROYED THEIR CAREERS—the worst of all punishments in a capitalistic society!

This issue over communism in liberal organizations became an early testing ground for future success in the American race for political power. Five members of JFK's cabinet were former members of AVC and voted the Communists out of left-wing organizations.

The way we decided on this issue determined the future of the members of my generation. I flunked this test for power sometime in late 1947 or early 1948. The chapter at the university voted on whether members of the Communist party should be allowed to keep their membership in AVC. I went to the meeting, but my heart was no longer in the organization; it offended me to deny others their rights, no matter what their political belief.

I dropped out of all political activity. I had watched people who had been good friends destroy each other, no longer speak. Careers were made on the stand one made on the Communist issue in the late 1940s and early 1950s. If that was the way to success, I could not follow it.

Between 1945 and 1948 the great dream of peace with justice that came from the war and our woundings was destroyed, in the West by our anti-Communist purges and in the East by Stalin's paranoiac need for self-defense: the beginnings of the Cold War.

Men who lied and cheated rose to power. McCarthy, who made his reputation on lies. Nixon, who came to power out of the House Un-American Activities Committee, whose chairman, J. Parnell Thomas, was later jailed for the misappropriation of public funds. Ronald Reagan, who helped lead the Screen Actors Guild into the anti-Communist camp.

Then the United States made a decision that still haunts our public life today: We must arm ourselves out of fear and rage, create defense departments, make hydrogen bombs, fight the Reds in dirty little rice paddies around the globe, prove our dominance in this world of enemies, beat those motherfucking Reds, the evil empire, the terror of the earth. We must "contain" our enemies through violence and the latest weapons technology, a theory of deterrence no different from that which had motivated my ten generations of ancestors on the killing grounds of America. The Kentucky rifle should have stopped wars, the plains rifle should have stopped wars *Colt revolver Gatling gun Winchester rifle Springfield rifle machine gun tank poison gas airplane napalm agent orange A-bomb hydrogen bomb lasers Star Wars.* Technology would always overwhelm our enemies if we spent enough, tested enough, researched enough. As if there were some need for us to have an enemy as part of our national character, unable to define ourselves without some dark shadow that we must always be fighting on the killing grounds of the world, using our most modern military technology.

By the time I was twenty-three or -four my world had become increasingly peopled with enemies. My father was no longer the giant I had worshiped as we sat in our boat by the artesian well that spouted fresh water into the salten sea. My country, no longer the land of freedom for which I had almost died, was now persecuting those I knew to be innocent. Worst of all, the USSR was killing its wartime heroes—wounded in the same war I was—in the Gulag, the Siberian death camps.

Peace and justice out of a war?

It was a joke.

My wounding was a joke. THE ONLY MAN IN THE WORLD WITH HALF AN ASS AND A HOLE IN HIS HEAD!

Men with rifles dominated the earth on killing grounds.

My wounding made no sense in a society of such injustice.

I quit school, fled down labyrinthine ways, went on the bum, hitchhiked through dirty little towns where dirty little men scoffed at me with my two-day beard and "no place of employment," only my veteran's compensation to keep me alive. I wrote in my journals on the banks of streams whose names I never knew, walked through towns at night so policemen would not question my right to be on their roads. I lay under the stars, alone.

CHAPTER 6

TAKING UP THE RIFLE

> *And men will not understand us—for the
> generation that grew up before us, though it
> has passed these years with us here, already had
> a home and a calling; now it will return to its
> old occupations, and the war will be forgot-
> ten—and the generation that has grown up
> after us will be strange to us and push us aside.
> We will be superfluous even to ourselves, we
> will grow older, a few will adapt themselves,
> some others will merely submit, and most
> will be bewildered;—the years will pass by and
> in the end we shall fall into ruin.*
> —Erich Maria Remarque
> *All Quiet on the Western Front*

Three years later in my one-room apartment in Green-
wich Village, I took my Purple Heart from its satin
case, carried it to the garbage can just before I moved
it to the street, dumped the medal into the mess of coffee
grounds, eggshells and busted beer bottles. All that day I
could see the glint of purple on the top of my garbage, sitting
on the curb outside. An old man came by and glanced at the
medal, picked it up, shrugged: it obviously had no value at the
local pawnshop. A horde of boys wandered by. One grabbed
the medal, threw it to a companion. For a moment they played
catch with that medal the officer had pinned on my chest in

England, until they grew tired of the game. One boy threw it at the can. It missed and fell to the street. No one bothered to pick it up. When the garbagemen came, they ignored it and, later that night, it was kicked into the gutter. I watched it lie there for two days. On the third it disappeared.

The meaning of my wounds had disappeared as the Cold War escalated. Not just internationally, where the Korean conflict raged. Not just in government—where McCarthy attacked innocent people, where Nixon got elected to the Senate in California on a smear campaign of anticommunism, where suicides intensified—but also in private life. *Red Channels* published names of suspected Communists in the communications industry who were then fired instantly. The Miss America contest proclaimed that young women had to be free of Communist taint. Libraries gave *The Grapes of Wrath* a red star because it spoke of iniquities in the nation. Our famous detective writer, Mickey Spillane, wrote: "I killed more people tonight than I have fingers on my hands. I shot them in cold blood and enjoyed every minute of it. . . . They were Commies . . . Red sons-of-bitches who should have died long ago." A member of the Indiana State Textbook Commission said, in utter seriousness: "There is a Communist directive in education now to stress the story of Robin Hood. They want to stress it because he robbed the rich and gave to the poor. That's the Communist line. It's just a smearing of law and order."

A viciousness made life in the United States ugly, claustrophobic. It seemed impossible to breathe. The USSR, under Stalin, had become even more repressive. Out of that war, for which boys my age had volunteered all over the world, had arisen an even greater rage and fear. My wounds, their wounds, had no meaning beyond deepest despair.

I had fled all public activity, but my private life was still as scarred by the impact of those wounds. I had not found a career and could not get my work published. I was unable to summon the energy to continue college, get a graduate degree, move into the future. I survived in New York on an endless round of part-time jobs: selling furs over the telephone, making change at an automat at Fifty-fifth and Broadway, investigating automobile accidents in Harlem for an insurance company. I had even considered the ministry, seduced by my mother's persuasion, but had quickly learned how little I worshiped her God, too saccharine for my harsh knowledge of war and killing grounds.

My flights had taken me to a year in Mexico, pursuing the image of Hemingway. Like him, I had fled the States to write, slowly expanding my journal into short stories and a novel, building on my experiences of the war. But my stories were of horror, not of romance; of cowardice, not of courage. I wrote a novel about a man who ran in battle, spent the rest of his life dealing with that fact, circling deeper into despair, then madness:

> *. . . Circles within circles, each one darker than before, he sank down into his pain, nothing but pain, as if he had been stripped of flesh and every nerve was exposed, pain like a drill scraping over his nerves, scraping, scraping, scraping, and some enormous face behind the drill laughing at his loss of manhood.*

I had no friends in New York. I wandered the streets alone, wrote, walked, thought, unable to reach out to those peers at the university who once had supported me, ashamed of this thing I had become: a man without a career, even a meaningful job, throwing nickels at the automat.

My marriage of two years was the only good event since leaving Chicago, although my failures had eaten away at that too. For a moment with my wife, I touched another human being in ways I never could have imagined, experienced a trust never felt before. Our relationship warmed me and broke, for a brief time, the emasculation that had haunted me since my wounding.

But I quickly learned that, when I desired to leave my mother for another woman, my mother could not let me go. My freedom and her maternity were in deepest conflict. Still, in the very core of our beings were the emotions we had explored for each other immediately after I returned home from France so broken and hurt. She pursued me with phone calls, visits—visits during which I became impotent, unable to make love with my wife, as though in my unconscious my wound had given my mother some immense power over me, still her child, her Eddie, the Eddie of her kisses.

After two years of marriage, years of flight, chaos, confusion in my deepest being, somehow my wife's love for me and mine for her still survived, some lingering memory of our first exploration of each other, our joy. My wife had stayed with me as I circled downward into failure; even now, though separated, we sometimes saw each other, either in this hovel in the Village or in her apartment on the Upper West Side, off Riverside Drive. An entry in my journal for those years still scrapes my nerves with remembered pain:

> *It always lies between us: whenever we walk, talk, eat. With friends, alone, apart, the strange, brooding shadow creeps silently behind us and, each night, as we turn to our beds, the enormity of our fear rises again. What would happen this night?*

That dark shadow was my mother, that dark shadow was my wound, that dark shadow was impenetrable blackness when the two combined, almost as if I sank into darkness. My wound bound me to my mother in ways I did not grasp, a dependence I did not want to understand, admitted by neither of us, my poor wife caught in a nightmare not of her making. My mother, out of her own pain, her despair over my wound, my father's increasing flight into power, had turned to me with all her beauty, desire and love. And I could not let her go.

So I fled down the darkening ways of emasculation and madness. I wandered through New York in the long, gray days and nights, alone, alone, seeing its other lonelies and lost: women on street corners selling their bodies; old men staggering to a drunken death in unknown alleys; brash young blacks and Puerto Ricans with their music in the subway laughing at me—me, a lost white boy, just one more New York crazy—strange young men, with wild and frightened eyes, driven by demons they did not understand.

Fear had seeped through that hole in my head into my whole being. My brain, my command center, had been obscenely penetrated, busted open, an unspeakable violation lying below the depths of conciousness. I lived in a growing terror of death. The snarl of a jet made me want to puke. I could no longer tolerate rational discussions; I blew up with sudden sharp rages. The sky above me seemed arched with threat as if always trembling on the verge of a thunderstorm.

I wanted to run.

But where could I turn?

To make matters more complicated, Dad and Mother now lived in the East. Dad had tracked down those relatives of his who remained in Blandford, Massachusetts—Cousin Fanny to whom Grandma Lydia Tiffany had written all those letters from Arkansas and Mississippi. It was remarkable that Fanny Tiffany DeBrall was still alive. Dad traveled to Blandford in the late 1940s, turned his charm on all those female relatives, using his wealth to impress them. He stayed in the home to which his grandmother had written from her purgatory in Mississippi, the Elysian fields of New England she remembered as a child. For him it was really the pinnacle of his power, to return north to the home his grandmother had dreamed about, her dream crucial to the mythology of his family.

The home in Blandford was a magnificent place. A tavern in Revolutionary War days, it still had many of the furnishings from that period. Sited on over eighty acres of lovely New England mountainside, it had a trout stream, fields of blueberries and—best of all—a virgin hemlock forest, trees over two hundred years old, majestic in their vaulted grace. To walk under them reminded me of the cathedral at Salisbury, its light and sublimity, where I had once experienced a moment of real peace.

Dad bought that farm (including all the antiques) from his relatives—at a cheaper price, I am sure, because he kept it all in the family—maintaining memories of a New England tradition of over two hundred years. He now owned his grandmother's heritage.

He named it "Eddywood." A sign at the driveway, stationery, envelopes, the pride of his brand upon the land. I froze with embarrassment, knowing little then of the family history, of Lydia's son, my grandfather, also named Eddie. It seemed to me that he had named the farm after me.

I knew that my parents bought the farm only to follow me east. In the deepest sense, neither Mother nor Dad would let me go. They had tried to enroll me in a college of their choice after I left the university. They constantly badgered me concerning a career. They pursued me down the ways of my madness. My parents still dominated me as if I were a little boy.

I finally came to the point where I could no longer tolerate seeing my mother. I refused her calls, her letters, her visits.

Dad often came to New York. I went out to dinner with him. I wore my one good seersucker suit. We ate. We tried to talk.

I suffered in his presence, the man I had so loved once.

I must have hurt him deeply. This boy he had taken on all those fishing trips, hunting trips. This boy scarcely a man, injured in the war, so lost, working at terrible jobs in this terrible city, unable to find himself, unable to accept any help from his father, totally, cruelly rejecting his mother, marriage a mess. This boy, his son—how he must have wanted to hold me, love me.

Yet I was terrified of his help.

Two men locked in a dark room, stumbling as they sought each other.

I always grew smaller when I was with him, asking that terrible question: WHO AM I?

And one night after we had had dinner, I took my red flannel bathrobe out of the closet, methodically slipped the belt from its loops, found a stool under the kitchen table. Yanking back my fingers from the heat, I tied one end of the belt around a hot-water pipe, stood on the stool, tied the other end around my neck. It seemed the only reasonable act to perform. Nothing was left.

Just six years before, when I returned to the States on that hospital ship, all Manhattan lay beneath me as I rose up through the hatch on that stretcher: I would own New York City, possess it. It would mark my power.

I wept great tears. I remembered my friends in Chicago, those I was unable to call, and felt overwhelmed by my failure and my guilt. I remembered my wife, the moments of trust we had known. I remembered how much I had loved the sky and the sea and the wind soft upon my flesh.

Finally, I stepped down from the stool, untying the belt from around my neck. My soul had resisted the killing of my body.

The next morning, through the mother of a friend I had known at the university, I located a psychiatrist.

The psychiatrist told me on my first visit that he planned on moving to rural Connecticut that summer and could not keep me as a patient in New York. It made no difference. I had come to hate the city. Now, for the first time since Chicago, I had someone who would listen.

On a June day in 1951 I hitchhiked to Connecticut. Suddenly out of the city where I had been such a failure, away from the marriage in which I could not function, out again into the country—the trees, the land, the sky, the water, the memory of my father, our moments outdoors together. That night, when it darkened, I stopped at a tourist home in Bethel. (Motels were then a thing of the future.) For the first time since leaving the University of Chicago I felt whole again.

In Oxford I found a small cabin on a hill overlooking the Housatonic River, two miles below Stevenson's Dam. It had electricity but no running water; I used the hand pump and the two-holer outside.

I spent the summer of 1951 there, totally out of contact with my father, my mother, my wife, the world, entwined in the pain of my wounding and all my failures.

I began to write again, every morning from eight to twelve. I worked every afternoon on a construction crew repairing the face of the dam. Its old concrete had rotted. We chopped out the bad concrete and replaced it with new. We used small air hammers that reminded me of the .45-caliber machine guns we had carried on guard duty in France. They shook our wrists and our shoulders when we pressed the triggers and released the compressed air.

I had no car then. I walked to work. Once a week I took the bus to Derby to shop. I brought my canned goods back to the cabin in an old Army rucksack. Three nights a week I walked to my psychiatrist's home after work. Two miles to the dam from my cabin. Four miles to his house. Six miles back after my fifty-minute hour.

By the end of the summer I had saved enough money to buy a 1938 Ford sedan.

That fall I moved into an apartment in Woodbury, on its main street. I found a job in a small factory in Southbury, making electronic switch boxes for the Navy to use in the Korean War. My wife and I even began to see each other again, a greater warmth between us as I began to understand the emotions that drove me.

Then . . . then my father and mother came back into my life. As if my independence, my development of my own values, my belief in social justice and my attempts to write, were enormous threats to their being.

They made forays from Blandford down to Woodbury, came to my apartment.

Finally my father asked to see my psychiatrist. They met. Even as I remember I wince inside.

Two men utterly different, incompatible. My doctor, I am sure, tried to protect me from my father, protect the integrity of his patient. Dad searched for his son, the one he had lost. I know now, a father myself with grown children, how much my rejection hurt Dad.

Four or five years passed before I saw him again.

He returned to Blandford and sold Eddywood. Not just sold it but, from some inward anger and rage directed (I am sure) at me for my rebellion and my desertion, destroyed the land around the house. He sold the timber rights to the hemlock forest so a lumber company would clear-cut that magnificent natural heritage. It was reduced to a chaos of stumps and slashed branches. He split the fields around the farmhouse into lots for development. Only a few acres of the original farm remained pristine and pure.

I never went back to that farm, the home of which Lydia Tiffany had dreamed, the home to which she had sent those letters. That farm of memory and purity was destroyed by her grandson, my father, its land lotted for development, its hemlock forest decimated, its trout stream drained. My last good feelings about my father had centered on how we had loved nature together. This act ended all that.

And yet my financial needs were great. Still unable to really work, still lost in terms of a career, I took his money. And loathed myself for taking it, loathed him for giving it.

I still absolutely refused to see my mother. I could not bear to be near my wife. Once more, as my journals indicate, I spiraled down into nothingness, my only contact with reality those sessions with my shrink.

The fact of my wound never entered the sessions. In that era, analysis had little to do with understanding physical trauma. Emotional reality was a function of the child and its relation to its parents.

In retrospect it seems almost impossible to believe that we never discussed the war. My doctor was not just a fine professional, he was an honest, kind and just man—"wise," that most hackneyed of words. Those characteristics of his personality attracted me, so different from the bombastic romanticism of my father, the Hemingwayesque worship of courage. If my shrink believed that the war had little to do with my condition, I believed him. If he believed that the feminine aspects of my character unmanned me, he must be correct.

I wrote in my journal:

May 1952

> *My doctor teaches me that if I am to ever get well, I must understand that deep within me, coming from my mother, is a passive, feminine part of myself, a latent homosexuality at complete odds with my masculinity. I must work my way through to my masculinity . . . only in my masculinity lies naturalness and integrity. . . . He confirms in me all the lessons about masculinity and femininity I learned as a child: THOSE JUICES WOULD WASH ME INTO NOTHINGNESS. YOU GOT TO BE A ROCK TO BE A MAN, BOY. GET THE WOMAN OUT OF YOUR SYSTEM.*

In the psychiatry of that day there were males and females, clear roles for each. A man must not admit the feminine in himself; a woman, the male in herself. A man's power lay in mastery, in work, control over the real world. Women had children and managed the home. To accept the feminine inside myself—the compassion of my childhood, a life outside of killing grounds—became an act of self-destruction.

My wound had first diminished me, made me ashamed of my sexuality. My mother had given me rest, surcease that filled me with guilt. Now the issue was no longer the wound but the shame, not the maiming but the guilt. The meaning of war, its nature, its barbarism, that long inheritance of violence from my forebears, the rifles of my fathers, the fact of killing grounds in this century of war were no longer important. In the oddest kind of way, my failure to discover a career, my continued dependence on Dad for money, my inability to publish became exclusively my fault. The failure of a society reeking with repression, a hundred years of war ending with the Holocaust, these were no longer part of the equation.

I buried deep within me all memories of that day in France, the fact of the wounding, the cathedrals at Reims and Salisbury.

I imagined I had an ax in my skull, splitting my brain in half. I felt it protruding from my head, driven deep into the hole that the shrapnel had first penetrated. The headaches—sometimes seconds, only seconds of vibration—made me feel mad with pain. (And the surgeon: *You've got a brisk hemorrhage now.*)

I lashed out at my mother, then my wife, ceaseless in my childish demands, cruel, vicious. My wife, I am sure, found it impossible to understand me, a person filled with such chaos, such sullenness, such rage.

My mother wrote to my father of her confusion and her pain:

> *La Grange, Ill.*
> *March 29, 1950*

> *. . . makes me feel sad. If I started being sympathetic about how much parents loved their children, etc., I would spend a lot of time thinking about us and Eddie. I do spend lots of time wondering why it happened to us but I try not to brood over it because it will not help the situation.*

> *Mobile, Alabama*
> *September 9, 1951*

> *I'm glad you could spend the weekend*
> *with Eddie and it made me feel fine to hear you*
> *say that Eddie was getting along all right. I*
> *hope you got to talk to the doctor in person.*
> *You will feel better about it then. Just let him*
> *know that you are willing to do whatever you*
> *can to help, but that you do not want to*
> *interfere.*

> *Ocean Springs, Mississippi*
> *April 19, 1952*

> *Well, you are with Eddie this morning*
> *and I do hope that everything is fine there and*
> *that your report will be an improvement over*
> *the past. . . . I'm praying that your visit with*
> *Eddie was all that you expected and that he is*
> *more like himself. . . . Do hope you will be able*
> *to report much improvement in Eddie's condi-*
> *tion. I mean his attitude toward everything . . .*

I supported myself by starting a lawn-care business in
Newtown: Wood's Lawn and Garden Service. I looked
after estates in the afternoons. In the mornings I mowed
lawns, weeded, planted shrubs. I continued to write.

My inherent love of nature slowly evolved as the fiber of
my being, brought back to life by the love of place, the New
England landscape of my ancestors: the sedate countryside,
granite slope of hills, cool caress of dew on plants in early
morning, the gratifying thrust of a spade into rich soil, gold
and scarlet leaves in the fall, wind whipping my flesh.

I found my first sense of God in nature. One day, I

remember, I sat with my lunch on a hillside in early spring, throwing bits of my sandwich to the jays hopping about me. The sky arched above my head, green leaves shimmered in the sun, splendor of the New England spring when new life bursts from dead wood and breezes riffle each budding leaf. I knew nature's eternity for a moment, beyond time, beyond space, knew I was part of it, bonded to it: this flesh, these bones, this heart would one day die and merge into this beauty, merge into boundless energy and matter.

For this instant I was not alone, I was unafraid of death and wounding.

Southbury, Conn.
October 1952

It is silence I seek, the silence of God . . .

I lived by my journals in those splendid days alone, used words to make some sense of my wounding and the war, the betrayal of my father and the loss of my many mothers. Words ordered my past, my childhood, my parents, the war, politics into some pattern of beauty. Beauty had its own meaning, related to living out of doors, working with my hands. I dropped out in rural Connecticut, a generation ahead of my time. I felt the first moments of sweet and gentle peace my life had known since my wounding.

I lived by some sense of God as well, the God of Reims and Salisbury and that hemlock forest, the God of those hemlocks. I heard of the Quaker's Peace Testimony, their commitment to nonviolence. I started attending their meetings, attracted by both the silence and the dedication to stopping wars and woundings. In the silence of those meetings I could rest. Eight or twenty people gathered to seek their God in common. They believed in the fundamental goodness of humanity. Each of us had an inner light. When we touched it, it gave us great joy. It spread to encompass the lonely and the suffering of the world.

I listened.

I longed to believe.

I needed to believe.

But in my depths lay a persistent uneasiness: how to relate this faith to the suffering I had seen? *La femme scalpée*? The men I saw killed? McCarthy? Stalin? Repression of the Cold War? Dad and his rape of the farm? My mother's arms still tight about me, refusing to let go?

Oh, I longed for a God of light and His embrace—but dared not accept a caress.

Wood's Lawn and Garden Service! I put in lawns and septic tanks, transplanted shrubs, mowed grass, weeded gardens, raked leaves. A handyman.

In winters I worked in factories: Plastic Molding Company and Fabric Fire Hose in Sandy Hook.

As I finally settled into some ordered pattern of living, rooted in art and nature and God, my wife and I started seeing each other again. Disastrous at first, we managed in time to rediscover some of that magic that had first brought us together. Our relationship improved. She left New York for Connecticut—and became pregnant. We were to have twins.

My children's birth marked a new era in my life.

After holding them the first time, I wrote in my journal: "So beautiful, skin so clear, blood just warm and red beneath its porcelain surface. They mew like kittens, wiggle like—like earthworms, that's what!"

I swelled with pride.

A boy and a girl. My wife nursed. I gave the night feeding with bottles. I laid them on the couch, rested the bottles on pillows, put the nipples in their open mouths. I held them, burped them, changed their diapers, put them gently to bed, once more a generation ahead of my time.

For a brief moment in the fifties we achieved a precarious balance, a way of life that satisfied us both. We bought a home, made friends, became part of the community.

The middle and late fifties were perhaps the best years of my life. McCarthy had been censured by the Senate. Internationally, there were no major wars. Domestically, life remained calm. I had dropped out of the booby hatch, struggling to make a life outside of killing grounds. Art was rimmed and framed by the natural world and my family. I worked outside each day in cold and heat, any weather, wet or dry. My fingers dug deep into harsh burlap, cracking my nails as I lifted balled shrubs for transplanting.

I came home to a wife and children, both of whom I loved. We owned a small house with an acre of land. I painted and hung shelves, fixed doors, built bookcases.

> *Patty-cake, patty-cake,*
> *Baker's man,*
> *Bake me a cake*
> *As fast as you can.*
>
> *This is the church*
> *And this is the steeple.*
> *Open the door*
> *And see all the people.*

My wife and I created a family of magic and mystery. A third child was born, and my delight was fully as great.

My parents and I even began to communicate again after the children were born. They came to see us. Dad sent us train tickets; we traveled south to where he retired (and where he was born), near Moss Point, Mississippi.

Deep within—from my doctor and my work in nature, the calming cycle of the seasons, my attempts to write—the memory of my wounding and the war were slowly forgotten, buried in the icy depths of my mind.

But still I had no money or career. My writing was always rejected: "Your work is good, Mr. Wood . . . but we can find no place for a novel that so denigrates patriotism and war. . . . " When people asked me at a party what I did, I would blush and stammer. A writer? Unpublished? A gardener? Handyman? Fingernails broken and black; I was ashamed of them.

WHO IN CHRIST'S SWEET NAME WAS I?

A wife and three children depended on me. I had less and less time for my writing. I now got up at four or five and wrote for two hours before rushing to work. The kids' need for space had squeezed out my study. I worked in cramped quarters in the basement, surrounded by garden tools and cow manure.

I needed a career of my own, some of my father's power for myself.

My psychiatrist had helped me learn down to the bottom of my bones that the feminine part of myself, the voices of my many mothers, my quest for social justice, my desire to write, must be relinquished if I were to become a successful male. My marriage forced me to become the rock on which my family rested. My childhood memories demanded I deny my female juices. My terror of my mother made it impossible for me to accept her compassion as part of my own being. Hemingway, the only male model I had who had been wounded, saw courage as the essential male value.

A man must live on killing grounds.

All my fathers were correct: what mattered to manhood was using one's rifle in victory. But if this were true, in the final, terrible analysis, if this were true, and I must finally join my ancestors as the eleventh-generation male to carry his weapon on the killing grounds of life, then I must do it on my own terms. Out of those values of social justice I had learned in the war and at the University of Chicago, out of my labor with my hands as a gardener, out of my anger at my father at destroying the landscape of the family farm, I must find my way. As with AVC, driven now by social purposes and also a love for the land, I would seek justice in society. Only this time I also wanted power.

One day in late 1957 I went out into our back yard and burned my manuscripts, written over ten years (including a novel about cowardice), saving only the poems and an unfinished novel about my mother's childhood. The next day I got in the car and drove to the University of Massachusetts, where I enrolled in the Department of Landscape Architecture. A year and a half later I was given a Sears Fellowship to the Massachusetts Institute of Technology to obtain a master's degree in city planning.

My career in public policy began.

PART IV

RENUNCIATION OF THE RIFLES OF MY FATHERS

WASHINGTON, D.C.
CAMBRIDGE, MASSACHUSETTS

[1959–1970]
1971–1974

YEARS OF POWER
IN KILLING GROUNDS

> *Power tends to corrupt; absolute power corrupts absolutely.*
>
> —Lord Acton

WASHINGTON, D.C.

SUMMER 1971

W hat is my life like as a consultant to the Department of Transportation, vice-president of one of D.C.'s prestigious research firms?

I talk on the telephone. Go to meetings. Write letters. Write reports. Write memoranda. Go to lunch, drink two martinis, talk some more.

Words. Words. Words. Words. What is the meaning of the words I now use? Are they only bullshit? No. Worse than bullshit. Bullshit has an earthy quality. It stinks. Steams. Fertilizes the soil. What I produce is reports, something no one ever reads. I've never yet talked to anyone who read a report from cover to cover unless it was required by the job. Reports are a function of our peculiar life-style, which has a ghostly quality. We are the mobile generation, rising from one economic class to another, moving from one city to another, seldom stable for more than two or three years, even always on the move from the places in which we temporarily live. For the airplane created a new way of life in the United States, different from the remainder of the Western world, built around modules that only connect to other modules.

In my office at 9:00 AM to stuff my briefcase, elevator at 9:05, taxi at 9:10, Washington National Airport at 9:30, its lobby frenetic with other "corpses." The airplane finally at 9:45, after sitting in a waiting room that contains no organic material, only plastic and nylon. Squeezed into my assigned seat, wondering what the fuck will happen if this plane crashes—especially when one flies a hundred thousand miles a year and has already experienced a couple of terrifying landings (the fear at the bottom, always the gut-wrenching fear: off the ground, get this thing off the ground, please, please, OH, PLEASE, GOD, GET THIS THING OFF THE GROUND!), then up in the air, watching the No Smoking sign, praying for it to go off, a cigarette already in the mouth. Then the same fear at the other end in San Francisco: get this thing on the ground, on the ground, OH, PLEASE, GET THIS THING ON THE GROUND!!! Another waiting room, another taxi, another office where I meet with strangers I don't know, don't like, would not even invite into my home for a drink, another taxi, another module, a cold room even if it *is* the St. Francis or the Fairmont.

And this is work?

Producing a product of which one can be proud?

Madness. Schizophrenia. Illusion. Fantasy.

A system built only for those who have never loved a place or a piece of land as home.

As I travel from great city to great city—Chicago, Denver, Dallas, San Francisco, Boston, Houston, Atlanta, Pittsburgh—I search for reasons we fail to save our land. We seek to save it through legislation and programs—yet, no matter which ones we select, we fail. We seek to save it by institutions—yet, no matter which ones we create, they fail.

It is our national character that is at fault. Some deep part of ourselves sees land only as a resource for development and profit. After all, was not our first national hero, George

Washington, a land speculator before he became our military leader and first president?

O urs is a nation dedicated only to profit. In the corporations for which I work, the bottom line is the only criterion for determining success or failure. If I make money, I can walk naked down Connecticut Avenue in the middle of the afternoon and corporate officers would only applaud: "There goes ol' Ed. Hell of a guy. Did'ja read his profit statement? He's a comer."

And if I lose money?

Banish him. Send him to North Dakota in January.

M y consulting work here is hugely successful, but it no longer deals with issues of race and equality, those social housing concerns I worked on before the death of Martin Luther King. Since his assassination, the country has turned to other needs. I now work on problems of transportation and the environment, the reason I came to our nation's capital. . . .

Bullshit. Bullshit. And bullshit again. This hypocrisy makes me want to puke. I came to Washington seeking power. I came to Washington seeking sex. These two ruthless masters drove my soul, almost as if I were out of control of myself, still running hard to make up for those lost years after the war when I spun into nothingness.

MIT catapulted me to success. I ran on sixty- and eighty-hour work weeks after I graduated, driven by inward compulsions, that strange combination of the search for social justice and the drive to achieve my father's power. Concern for social improvement glowed in the 1960s with the programs of Jack Kennedy and Lyndon Johnson. Poverty programs. Model city programs. Housing programs. We would remake the world, have "the lion lie down with the lamb."

But with the assassination of Martin Luther King in 1968 and the election of Richard Nixon as president, society's commitment to social change collapsed. Oh, I could have continued to fight for those values of justice and equity, but instead, at the first opportunity, I came to Washington, determined to pass my peers, repressing the memory of my wound, pursuing the power my father had achieved, power to spend money, buy the things he had always bought for me.

And I wanted the women I knew he had possessed, the Ladies of Storyville. I longed for the sexual exploration I had missed as child and youth, unable to seek it out because of that gaping hole in my ass. I was driven now, out of control, determined, beyond understanding, to make up for what I had lost. *PlayboyHustlerScrew* of the sixties with the mini-skirts and hot pants on the street and swinging hips and movies like *La Dolce Vita* and *Blow Up* telling us to take it and make it and use it. Fucking became the end of life in the sixties in America: *PlayboyHustlerScrew* with the centerfold's shyly virginal face and her red-nailed fingertip reaching down into her triangle of hair, not staring wearily innocently like the Lady of Storyville but fingers opening and exploring the pearly cunt as if it contained the end and goal of life, all being and all meaning wrapped up in its wet and shining smooth-ness, cunt and cock and orgasm the essence of our era: oh fuck and fuck and fuck. What the kids talked about and did, what my generation was told it had missed: the free woman of the sixties, the woman I was told was my right. Find her, seize her, take her, her breasts, her rose-nippled breasts, her lips reaching up and taking my own, my hands to her shoulder, deep into her flesh, holding her rising breasts, a cry repressed upon her lips. Her lips suck me, hold me, fingers claw into my back, her body over mine and under mine. Men and women of the sixties, suddenly freed by the pill to do their thing, the first generation in the history of humanity that no longer needed to fear pregnancy, freed by technology. The sixties with their pornographic movies where a man had sex with two women, fucking one while he sucked the other's tits; where two women went down on each other; where a man fucked a woman in the ass; where a woman sucked off a man, lapping his big fat cock as if they both were dogs, eating the salty jism when he came. The sixties with cunt and cock and orgasm the training grounds for the future leaders of America (while in Vietnam poor whites and blacks died for the nature of our sins). The sixties when good middle-class kids flocked to Washington to protest, crying, "ONE. TWO. THREE. FOUR. WE HATE YOUR FUCKING WAR!!!" And when I tried to get a room at the Mayflower for my clients, the hotel was full of kids in dirty jeans using their father's credit cards to pay for their rooms. The sixties, power and sex. I wanted 'em both. And, sure, I did the other things, tried to make a better world, but all desires were wrapped together and I wanted 'em ALL.

My wife was smart enough to see through me. "Power, Ed. Power. You've become like your father at last. He waited a long time, but he's got you now." I hated her for those words.

The forces driving me to emulate him, have his perks, play his games with women, were like great driving jets pulsing in my mind. Out of control of myself in the deepest sense of the word, probably half mad with desires never achieved, I left my family, broke the most primeval trust.

How can I describe that insatiable need? Stored up, banked inside me since the day of my wounding, since coming home to my mother, only partially freed by her death in 1962, it had simmered all these years.

Now I am afire. But the oddest thing has happened. I can still only burn, unable to act, locked into a mighty prison of my past, my wound, my mother, the bars that contained me. The moment I had real power, I suddenly knew it for what it was: an insatiable demand never fulfilled. The moment I knew I could have that sex, another cosmic joke was played upon me. I still could not expose that scar except in the frame of love. My wound and the conflicts resulting from it have never been resolved.

Yet now I have left my family, grievously injured my children, and I live in the killing grounds of Washington. Alone.

I can still remember when Washington was a sleepy southern town. Dad brought me here when I was a child.

We stayed at the old Willard and ate with our congressman at the Occidental Restaurant next door.

The buildings then had a human scale as if built by men. Now? The high-rise office buildings have a biscuitlike quality as if pressed from the same mold. Government, perhaps all modern architecture, seems to be produced by a committee, the final product the combined idiocy of each committeeman's mind. Windows do not open to fresh air; organic material is forbidden. I choke.

Even the people possess this same faceless quality as if, like the tide, they are washed through the city every two years, flotsam of those unwilling or unable to return to their roots.

When people and buildings combine, especially in these great offices that house the government's bureaucracies, like the Department of Transportation where my clients work, all humanity is lost. My flesh feels pinched when I walk down those endless neon-lit corridors as if I myself, at last, were dead.

And when I walk down the city's streets alone at night, I leap from street lamp to street lamp, frightened in the dark that a great and unknown hand will reach out and yank me into all eternity.

I live in the press of power. Each day I feel as if soon I will be squeezed into nothingness. On one side of me the implacable force of the highway lobby, determined—determined, by God!—that it will pour that cement. On the other side, a small minority of environmentalists and blacks who want to stop expressways in America, believing that there are other solutions to our way of life than the automobile, the development it creates, the damage it does to our resources, physical and human.

What I work at with these groups is so important, perhaps the last chance we have in the nation to change our land-use pattern to some sensible form of life. We hope to shift transportation, at least some of it, from the automobile and the airplane back to the light-rail system, the bus, subways, even railroads, old forms of transportation, even European forms of transportation, forms of transportation that create centers, places of high density, places that can become real communities, lived in by all kinds of people, old, young, poor, rich, white, black. Real neighborhoods where people work and live and play and trust each other, places of work and play and residence, not those vast commuting suburbs, based on the automobile and the expressway, with low densities and two-generation households where there is no community and no stability. We fight against these developments, yet I sense that they are the nation's desire, the consumption of goods and services that goes with suburbia—a pattern that destroys our precious land, corrupts our air with pollution, making us dependent on the Middle East for oil, as if, like my father, our national character demands growth and development, the consequences be damned!

The system in which I live has no mercy. The men who run these great bureaucracies accept no opposition to their rule.

The laws of the firefight and the killing ground prevail in these windowless offices. Get that motherfucker before he gets you. Cut off his balls. You own 'em if you squeeze his nuts and shove it up her crack.

As if all men—and now women!—were strictly each other's enemies.

And this is government?

This the country for which I almost died?

It is a world of ruthless competition where each man and woman is only out for himself or herself. Each carries a rifle and is ready to use it as required. The only criterion for determining success is money—profit! or power—the amount of control one has over others.

There is no place for truth in Washington but only the vicious struggle to maintain and expand one's place in the pecking order.

I remember those moments when we came here in the 1960s to fulfill a dream, heard Martin Luther King sing his hymn of love: "I have a dream . . ." That voice, that honey-sweet voice stilled now by a rifle. The rifles of my fathers had once more slain the dream of a world without enemies, a world free of killing grounds, just as they had killed the dream for peace and justice after World War I and World War II. Killed not just Martin Luther King but all those other leaders for civil rights and equity—Jack Kennedy, Goodman, Chaney, Schwerner, Medgar Evers, Malcolm X, Bob Kennedy. Killed yellow men and women and children in Vietnam. As if there is some dark paranoia in the American soul that sees enemies in the day and dreams of them in the night, a paranoia that fears freedom for blacks and minorities and women and third-world nations and that must use violence to contain them. Dear God and sweet Jesus, what is there in the American heart that must kill and destroy? Is this my true and only inheritance, the rifles of my fathers my only way of life?

Everyone here is afraid. The men and women who work for the men of power exist in an atmosphere of fear. It penetrates one's pores, soaks one's skin, haunts one's dreams, a moral miasma, a fog choking, engulfing, threatening each moment in the day and in the night. It breeds men and women who live in constant paranoia, seeing only enemies, frightened that their program or their office, their salary, desk or secretary will be taken from them.

Then, without those perks, like my father, they would be nothing. Nothing without the props and artifacts they must own. So they must build more things to prove their power.

Expressways. Great downtowns. MALLS. Goddamn malls. The invention of Americans, our contributions to the world's architecture. (Dad loved them.)

Tear down slums. Destroy small businesses. Move blacks.

Consume to prove oneself. Clothes. Gadgets. Food. My God, the food! Ghiradelli Squares and Larimer Squares and Quincy Markets, not only meat markets where men and women sell themselves and exchange their flesh but places for mouths and tongues and juicy saliva. American food. Chinese food. Mexican food. Juicy hamburgers with red gravy sopping into the bread; pies, pies with apples piled three inches high over crust that crumbles in the mouth; fudge, thick and black and creamy; salads, all kinds of salads, all kinds of dressings, Russian and Blue Cheese and Italian and Thousand Island and Ranch; pancakes, piles of pancakes floating in melted butter.

We build these mausoleums and consume these goods while the people of colored nations starve, denying our death, masking our decline, living off their destruction.

FEBRUARY 1972

I've worked out an arrangement with MIT.

I can leave this job that is such a failure to work for the Planning Department, half-time teacher, half-time administrator. Perhaps I can escape this madness of competition and feel constructive in an ordered world?

CAMBRIDGE, MASSACHUSETTS

SEPTEMBER 1972

I've left the world of Washington for this job at MIT. Will I escape killing grounds here?

B ut in God's sweet name, what do I see? The hall in front of my office is only one more killing ground. Teachers and students swirl before these doors as if MIT were but another medieval court in France. Each might be carrying a rapier and a stiletto, ready to leap at an enemy. Compatriots and peers walk through the hall, carelessly stepping over those who have been slain, dragged to the garbage heap by menials.

Men and women fight for tenure, for parking spaces, offices, secretaries as if they were animals.

In the classes I teach, student interest centers only on technique. They want to know only *how* to do it. Why? That intellectual and gentle humanism in which I was bred at the University of Chicago has no meaning to this generation.

Thoughts for them have no precision unless they are numbered. Computers allow them to manipulate large amounts of data. Technique and data have but one goal: control of some technology so as to achieve power.

How different from the killing ground of the battlefield?

The assumption here at MIT is that the intellect contains the only reality of existence. Life is a function of theoretical brilliance or skill. Human beings therefore have no real meaning; they are merely pawns to manipulate for larger political or economic goals. No wonder the plans for the Vietnam War were the concepts of a Kissinger, a Rostow or a McBundy: they learned their trade in academia.

There is no real leadership here at MIT. No understanding of reality. No grace under pressure.

These people can only manage data. They believe that the massing of information can save them from perdition.

MIT's Sloan School of Management, Harvard's School of Business, Stanford's School of Business—I do believe that these people would still collect data while their throats were being cut.

September 7. I was wounded twenty-eight years ago today. For all these years I have carried the weight of that wound, seeking to understand its meaning, the meaning of the violence in which I have lived, which I see around me, MIT and Washington nothing but replicas of the killing grounds of combat.

I live in the jungle of the American people, who are incapable of overcoming their darkest impulses so as to live in a dream, in simple protection of the land and full love of our nation and all its people.

A dark paranoia lies at the heart of the American soul— a need for killing grounds, enemies, rifles.

September 26. I've just had a long-distance phone call. Dad died early this morning. Four hours ago. A massive heart attack.

My God! What is happening to my world?

* * *

OCEAN SPRINGS, MISSISSIPPI

When I reached Dad's home in Ocean Springs, there were cars parked in the driveway of his house and on the road and on the lawn, a great outpouring of grief. I pushed open the gate to the back yard, nodded to faces I remembered with names I could not place.

There on the lawn by the kitchen door I saw Mary Lou, the family maid. Tears wetted her old black face. Her heavy arms that had cooked for us and ironed our clothes and dusted our furniture as she laughed at my father's jokes and ministered to my dying mother—her heavy arms reached up to me, pulled me down to her side.

She tried to talk, kneeling on the grass, lifting her white apron above her head as if to fan away her grief.

"Mistuh Eddie!" she wailed. "Mistuh Eddie! Yo' daddy is dead."

She waved her apron again.

I fell into her open arms.

We hugged.

I stepped inside the door and my family was there, faces older now, worn, aunts and cousins and uncles I had not seen for years. They swept me into their bosom again. Had I ever been away?

Decisions after that. When the funeral? What price coffin? How many people for dinner after? What food would we serve?

On and on and on, until that night I stood by the open coffin in the funeral parlor and shook hands with several hundred people, some of them black, a miracle, for this was only 1972. "We loved yo' daddy, Mistuh Eddie," one of them murmured to me, holding my fingers in his gnarled hand. "He was mighty good to everybody, us colored folks too." Old and white, young and black, male and female, soft hands, worn hands, eyes wet with tears, faces open with sympathy.

The next day was even harder as I stared over the bayou at the back of the house, its live oaks and gray moss, its saw grass, stretching out toward Biloxi Bay.

Tears scalded my eyes.

A part of my life had ended.

I would not hear his cry again. I would never know again the magic of his smile. I would not hear him murmur at the end of our phone conversations, "God bless you, Eddie."

We had not really talked since our canoe trip in Canada in June 1944, just before I went overseas.

Sobs shook my chest. I seized my aunt and cried so hard I bit down into her shoulder to stop my tears.

Later that night, after the funeral, I got drunk by myself in his home. I walked around the rooms, touched his furniture, the phone from which he called me, his desk. I opened the drawers; the insurance policies were stacked neatly for me to take. I could still almost touch him.

When? Three nights ago we had talked; he complained about chest pain.

My father. Dead?

The force that had dominated my life. Dead?

I remembered the morning of his death, three days before. I had lain awake in my bed in Cambridge, long before dawn, vaguely aware of how much my chest hurt. For an instant it was almost impossible to breathe. Then I turned over and slept. I learned at six o'clock that morning that Dad had died of a massive heart attack at the same moment I woke, my chest paining. Our bond of love and hate that close. Fifteen hundred miles apart, my body sensed his pain.

I loved him so. I hated him so. The father who had given me his rifle when I was a boy, the father who had wounded me, the father I had denied for these many years.

Sometime in the night I stopped drinking and walked down to the bay. The moon was full, wind soft upon my cheeks with the warmth of autumn, a woman's lips gently caressing my skin.

I thought of him and all his magic and his pain and his wonderful joy, and I sobbed for all I had missed over the years. What had happened to the love I once felt for him, the giant of my childhood, who swirled me around his head, took me out of the house to see the stars brilliant in the purple sky?

I lay on the beach and cried until there were no more tears.

Before I left, I filled a small glass bottle with sea water and sand from that beach. It still sits on my desk.

CHAPTER 8

RETURN TO THE PAST

> *Time present and time past*
> *Are both perhaps present in time future,*
> *And time future contained in time past.*
> —T. S. Eliot, *Burnt Norton*

Two years after Dad's death, late one October evening, I returned to my apartment in Cambridge, Massachusetts, where I still followed my profession as a city planner. I paid the taxi driver, took out my bags, started up the steps of the old, wooden building where I lived. At the door I fumbled in my pocket for my keys.

A voice murmured behind me. I turned.

A black boy—he could not have been more than sixteen—stood by the porch banister. Something glinted in his hand.

It did not register for a moment. In his hand under the porch light, a pistol, small, like a .32-caliber revolver. He lifted it from his side. Shoved it hard in my belly.

"Wallet, mistuh. Gimme yo' wallet."

I thought it was a joke. Halloween?

But his gun was in my gut, hard, the tip of the barrel twisting through my shirt to my flesh.

"Gimme yo' wallet. Gimme it, I said!"

I flinched. My hand trembled; the index finger on my right hand twitched spasmodically.

This was my home. Things like this only happened in the movies, didn't they?

I stabbed my hand into my coat pocket. Almost dropped my wallet as I pulled it free.

The boy grabbed it. He shook it open and counted the money. I had over fifty dollars in small bills.

"Paper bills," he insisted. "Gimme yo' paper bills."

"That's all," I croaked, yanking out a handful of change and shoving it toward him.

He struck my hand away. The coins scattered over the porch floor. A quarter rolled toward the steps.

"Paper bills . . . paper bills . . . paper bills . . ."

A litany from his lips, eyes that examined me, impersonal, cold. Was it a second, a minute, an hour he stared at me?

Then suddenly he was gone, back into the night from where he came. Only the twisted cloth of my shirt, the coins scattered over the floor, the trembling of my hands, nausea in my stomach testified to his presence.

Later that night, much later, after the police had departed, I sat on the edge of the bed, the one that had been mine as a child, shuddering convulsively.

A noise outside my room? The boy back again?

I jerked upright. Fumbled in the closet. Dad's rifle, the one I had shipped north after his death. I yanked it from behind my jumbled clothes. Opened the leather case. Slid it out. The stock was still warm to my fingers, the barrel cold to my hand.

I found shells in Dad's old hunting jacket.

The bolt slid easily backward as it had when I was a child; the shell in my fingers rammed smoothly into the chamber as when we had hunted for deer. I slammed the bolt and clutched my father's rifle even closer to my chest.

How different my hands were from his, I thought. My fingers were not as fat, knuckles not as broad. The back of my hands lacked the brown liver spots. I felt the nick on the stock where I had slammed it into a rock, crawling through a fence as a boy.

I remembered those autumn days when the air stretched with perfect clarity up to the enormous dome of the sky. On cold winter mornings we piled into Dad's car and drove to

southern Illinois, where we searched for quail. The wing-
beating, hard-driving silhouettes burst up from the low scrub.
I swept my .410-gauge shotgun easily, caught and passed a
single, rising bird. I hardly felt the recoil as I saw it collapse,
explode in a puff of feathers, tumble toward the earth.

Where had it all gone?

Dad and Mother were dead, my marriage had deterio-
rated under the pressures of my drive for power, the land I
loved was growing more polluted each hour, our struggle for
social and racial justice in the sixties had petered out.

I had achieved all the power I desired, the top of my
profession. I had emulated Dad in my pursuit of worldly
goods. Even now, after my divorce, I had this apartment, a
home on Cape Cod, plenty of travel, kids in good colleges.

But what did it mean?

Nations still killing grounds.

Communities and cities now killing grounds.

Business, government and academia now killing grounds.

Families killing grounds as well.

M y work was the greatest killing ground of all. Trust
anyone in Cambridge or Washington? They'd cut off
my balls and stuff 'em in my mouth; they'd bury their own
mother alive for tenure, money, power.

And in my pursuit of power, my personal life had
disintegrated, my marriage ending in a horrendous divorce
that hurt the children I love so much. My work in killing
grounds had left no time for family. Even on family vacations
to the Maine woods, I would fly home to meet on problems
of policy. I ceded my fatherhood to my wife.

Power, baby, power.

My sixty-, eighty-hour weeks left no time for nature. My
work in killing grounds left no time for creativity; these days
I wrote nothing but reports, reports probably no one reads.
My work in killing grounds left no time for God. I never
thought of His existence.

Had not the whole world become a permanent killing ground since the end of World War II? How many wars? Four hundred? How many deaths? We arm with atomic bombs. We fight dirty little wars in undeveloped nations, selling them arms no longer sophisticated enough for our use, seizing their resources for our own. Communities pour their money into police departments, struggling to stop the constant rise of murder, rape and robbery on our streets. We read of gang rapes, murder done only for pleasure, even shown, live, on the screen. Fear of terrorists haunts our nights and days. Even cohabitation has become a killing ground; we have the easy option of killing what we make while it still is in the womb.

Carry the rifles of my fathers.

Own. Ravish. Control.

Protect myself against my enemies, grind them into the earth.

Wounds are nestled into wounds, scars compounding scars, as I flee down the nation's darkened streets and alleys, these great and monstrous suburbs in which I will be forever lost, always seeking succor, some place of rest, some tenderness, not even my nuclear family left to support me, not that great family that once held me, comforted me, warmed me as a child.

All supports blown apart, blown apart by all those deaths and losses, blown apart by all our migrations, blown apart by all the social changes, by technologies that allow us to do our own thing and find our pleasure without responsibility for its results, blown apart by free sexuality and easy divorce. Now that the family I once had is decimated, I too, like most of my peers, live alone in my cubicle, separated from others by age and sex and race.

What sense is there to this life?

Better to be dead? I tried to commit suicide once. Why not again? Only this time complete the act.

I feared my father's rifle in my hands. I feared it represented what the world has become since the end of World War II, killing grounds our only way of life, not even the family left as protection for our children. Should I now use this rifle to protect myself? Wound others as I was wounded? Or suck its cold nipple as my final solution?

I stumbled to the phone, but knew no one to call. I wept. I thought of how I would fail myself and my children if I used this rifle in self-destruction or turned it upon another.

Morning came.

Still I carried a loaded rifle.

The deeper I penetrated into pain, the closer I came to long-forgotten memories before the war and my wounding, before my years as a man, so dim that grasping them required me to shred away all that I had become, returning to that lost childhood, back and back and back before I knew of my father's rifle, before I was wounded, before I tore myself from both my parents, destroying them in my rage, before I entered the killing grounds of life, hearing once more those ancient voices, warm as once they had been, voices that cried like prophets and sang like angels. My mother: Was I warm at night? My stomach full? Did I sleep without fear? My father: Keep your word. Be a man, my son. Aunts and uncles, grandmothers and grandfathers, cousins, kissing cousins and cousins once removed, the voices of my mothers, those who believed in compassion, in God and charity and faith, spoke to me again, even though I had not listened to them for many years and did not remember when I heard them as a child. Did they speak at meals? Or at night as I lay asleep? Or in the morning as I left for school? Or on those weekends with Dad and all his friends as we fished and hunted? Or was it in church on Sunday morning? Or was it in the air, some subtle essence that penetrated my soul, a permanent part of my being?

I did not know, but I did remember as the pain clasped around my chest, did remember how some of them, the best, believed that humanity could survive any test: failure, loss, desertion, fear, betrayal.

Deep, deep, deep, oh as deep as the salten sea, lay memories of that lost childhood when ancient voices cried to me like prophets or sweet angels. A gift from the past as I cradled Dad's rifle in my lap, a warmth in the room like some ineffable caress, denying the absurdity and corruption in which I now lived, the dream, the land, my family alive again in my mind as pure as once they had been.

My fingers slowly slipped from the rifle stock. I still loved the land and longed for its embrace: *remembering* black swamp water in the bayous, crested waves curling on the beach, the bow wave as we slammed through a thunderstorm to the wharf and harbor. I longed for those years, those days and nights in Elysian fields, before the war and wounding, before the rifles.

What if I should go back to the South? Taste warm salt air? Wander through Springhill, Mobile, Bayou la Batre, Coden, Moss Point, Ocean Springs. See New Orleans, where Dad grew up, New Orleans of the turn of the century. Storyville and sin, bethels and born-again, the New Orleans that shaped my father into the man he became, the New Orleans whose women with sweet tongues and soft flesh and steel hearts created Dad's landscape of love as mother, whore and wife, especially the women of his family who held power and created places for their children free of killing grounds.

Once more I must rise and feel the wind upon my flesh and watch it waken the sleeping sea. A journey deep into my past . . . a way to understand, perhaps, at last, why my life has been such a failure. Why I still carry a rifle cradled so tightly in my arms, why my life has ended so alone, locked into this apartment by myself. How we, as a society, destroyed the dream of equity, devoted ourself to the building of weapons and the waging of war, how we destroyed our land, how our communities and cities have become places of great fear. How my career has become a joke, making me a pimp to developers.

A journey into my past to make sense of my present and my future.

The car is packed, windows shut, gas turned off, paper stopped. I sit for a moment in the living room. I finished my last meeting at work yesterday. A client from Washington had flown to meet us and discuss a report we were preparing. His review of our work was splendid. But what did it really mean? One more report that no one in government really acted upon, an exercise in futility in terms of changing public policy, about as useful as toilet paper. On the trip I must decide what to do about my career, the one in which I once had tried so hard to believe.

. . . I am feeling reluctant to depart.

My apartment remains a cave into which I can still retreat. It holds the few things I have salvaged from my marriage and the goods I inherited from my father. I am safe and secure inside its four walls. No one can get at me, not with the door bolted by the new locks I had placed on the frame since being robbed.

What can I expect to find on this trip back in time? Am I crazy? Should I stay here with my father's rifle in my closet to protect me, stay here where I am safe?

No, I will leave.

I stand and look around the room, note the rich sheen of the captain's chest into which I have placed all the family papers I have inherited: Lydia's letters; the other letters; papers going back to 1637, tracing our family history.

I feel troubled as I walk toward the car. As if something in the apartment left behind me contains a threat.

My shoulders hunch. My footsteps slow. I turn and stare at the gray clapboard building.

What broods there in my rooms, a presence ghostly and unknown, demanding that I return? I cannot leave until I find it.

Under the bed. Living room. Dining room. Kitchen. *The closet.*

The rifle's brown leather case gleams in the gray afternoon light. I am compelled by some emotion I cannot understand to reach down and lift it in my hand. I must take it with me on my journey south.

I carry it to the car and place it carefully on the seat beside me, patting it gently before I start up and drive toward Logan Airport.

The plane has settled into its flight pattern for the trip to New Orleans. My seat belt is off. I've bought a martini; it tastes sooooo good, as if, now, for the first time since that boy shoved his .32 pistol into my belly I'm beginning to relax, as if the night he robbed me long-repressed emotions exploded into my conscious mind, emotions first exposed after Dad died. Now, at last, I must deal with the rifle Dad left me, the killing grounds in which I have lived for twenty years, the wounding I received as a boy, all these traumas of my life suppressed for so long but, now, rising up to scourge me, memories always present, even if repressed, ready to strike at me in my family, in bed with a lover, at work, even within the walls of my own home.

Dad's rifle lies in the baggage compartment beneath me. I've checked it through.

Its presence on this plane both exhilarates and terrifies me. Exhilarates because I am protected from my enemies; no son of a bitch will ever rob me again. Exhilarates because there is such pleasure in owning and using a good weapon, handling it, oiling the stock, ramming a patch down the rifle barrel, the cloth twisting into machined grooves, holding one's thumbnail in the breech to search in reflected light for dirt. Yet it terrifies me because its use in killing sickens. Terrifies because of the memory of my wound; terrifies because of the fear, the gut-wrenching fear that someday I might turn it upon myself.

I must discover some meaning to my life.

I grow sleepy at last. Perhaps I shall dream?

I dream. Not of power or killing grounds. I dream of those great cathedrals of my youth, ones I had seen in the war, Reims and Salisbury. I dream of the cathedrals I had seen on my trip to Spain to meet my daughter in 1974: Lugo, Santiago de Compestella and Leon. I rest in those great vaults again, know peace in the beauty and delight of those stained-glass windows. Once again I even hear the soft choir of my mother's many voices, murmuring, murmuring . . .

I awake refreshed.

Might I yet find tenderness and meaning?

Yes. The road south is the road of my ancestors and, now, I travel it again, the last leg of this long journey home.

Two years. Two years since his death and the closing of his estate. Perhaps I can deal with it at last, not only those family papers that lie in his study at home, but with all the emotions that seared my consciousness at his death.

Yes, the road south is the road of my ancestors, and now I travel it again.

Remembering remembering Atlanta, when Mom and Dad and I drove down those muddy-red roads and the farmers in those nameless rural counties scattered nails to pierce our tires so they could fix the flats; *remembering remembering* all those county seats we drove through on Saturday afternoons when whites walked on one side of the square and blacks on the other and, even then, at eleven or twelve years of age, I could sense the violence that hung in the air as heavy as the sticky heat; *remembering remembering* the segregated streetcars we rode and the signs FOR COLORED ONLY on every public space we saw or touched.

Remembering, as the plane hurtles south.

I've just finished lunch. Beneath me the Allegheny Mountains are beginning to lift their sharp ridges from the Virginia plains. This is the land my ancestors conquered, carrying their rifles, just as I still carry mine today.

We were the first nation in the history of the world where the ordinary man could own a weapon, hang it over the fireplace, use it to kill game, defend himself and his family, fight for his territory and his rights. More than any other technological invention, the rifle gave us our power and our freedom.

I sag back in the seat and stare at the earth unfolding beneath me. I think of the weeks and months and years it took Peter Zachary to migrate over the distance I had already flown, two generations to accomplish what I had traveled in less than two hours.

Their world was not mine.

Their enemies were not mine.

Rain and cold and snow and forest and stream and dampness and Indians and British and sudden violent murder and passionate embrace—the earth of my fathers.

And yet . . . what was the difference between the rifle I carry on this airplane and the Kentucky rifle of Peter Zachary?

South and west from New England lay the road of my ancestors; the road my father followed on his vacations to the Gulf Coast from the North after the Depression; those family reunions in Bayou la Batre and Coden; the road of my great-grandparents, Oliver and Lydia Wood; the road of my grandfather, Edward Daniel Wood, born en route; the road of the Lombards, the Watsons, the Greens. The road south is my father's road. Baltimore. Washington. We stayed with my aunt in Tidewater, Virginia, after Dad's brother deserted her in 1938, the first hemorrhage in our family stability. The Shenandoah beyond her home—narrow two-lane highways designed with a grace unknown to our modern expressways.

The road rolled before us: North and South Carolina. Dad's big hands tight on the steering wheel, his lips sucking wetly upon his cigar, open as he hummed his favorite song, "Bye, Bye, Blackbird," his foot hard on the accelerator, fifty, sixty, seventy miles an hour (we once drove from Chicago to New Orleans in eighteen hours, over nine hundred miles), out into the other lane, calculating the distance within inches, swerving back into our lane, blare of truck horn swirling behind us, blast of hot fuel whipping around my face. The road south before us: Atlanta with its old Army post, Montgomery with the Confederate capitol, Bay Minette. Then, just before Mobile Bay, the restaurant where we always stopped.

A black man (a "darkie" back then) stood outside its weathered façade. He leaned just over the edge of the road, a huge brass bell clasped in his black hands.

"Cap'n! Cap'n!," he screamed at each passing automobile. "Come on in, Cap'n. Bes' ol' fried chicken in the state of Alabam'. Come on in!"

Dad always stopped. And even though months had passed since the last trip, the man's face would open with a cavernous grin.

"Why, Mistuh Wood," he cried. "Mistuh Wood, where yo' been? Seems like jus' yestidy yo' been here. Mighty fine pleasure seeing yo' again. Mighty fine pleasure!"

Dad always gave him a dime, grinning with condescension. (That was big money then.)

After eating, we drove across the steel-magic bridges stretched over Mobile Bay with the marsh grass at the sides of the roads waving above the car roof in the wind. I could smell the salt-muddy flats and see their darkness stretching toward the brown bay water with a freighter etched upon the horizon. Out over Mobile Bay, out Old Shell Road, past "nigger town," out and up the hill, past Springhill College on our left, farther up the hill, almost a red-dirt road now, oyster shells on the shoulders gleaming in the late afternoon sun, and there— there, just ahead, I see the weathered, unpainted fence up the hill, around the curve, and then Grandma Green, her old face wrinkled and round and firm, a smile of welcome full upon it.

With my mother and my father and his brother, Uncle B. C., then later my wife and our children after we moved to Connecticut, driving the Connecticut Turnpike to the Tappen Zee Bridge and the Garden State Parkway which ate quarters as if they were food, the New Jersey Turnpike with its industrially brutalized landscape, flaring metal towers and flaming refineries. . . . Yes, the road south is the road of my ancestors, and now I follow it again, seeking to understand who I am, what we are to become in our diminished future:

from Maine's gnarled boulders and Cape Cod's sandy beaches to Maryland's red clay and Mississippi's eroded loam, the romanticism and religion of the South, the narrow puritanism of the North, the dark violence of the rifles of my fathers my most fundamental inheritance as an American male.

The plane drones farther south and along the coast toward New Orleans, the Gulf islands white as bones beneath me, and I think I see the islands of my childhood, and in my memory Dad and I are anchored by the rusty pipe.

Then the plane begins its low descent over Lake Pontchartrain (where Uncle B. C. once killed a hundred ducks in less than two hours) and now, at five thousand feet, I see the tree moss and the sharp white specks of the egret, an exclamation point against the green swamp water. Down and down and down, the plane flat in its final glide, the shadow of the wheels rising to kiss the rubber tires, a bounce, a reverse thrust.

Dad should be here, Dad with his cigar and his brown-spotted hands and his hat pushed back and his delighted cry: "Eddie! Eddie! Over here, boy. God! So good to see you." With his big Oldsmobile and the air-conditioning and the stories, the old family stories rolling immediately from his lips.

I believed I did see him for a moment, and knew him and remembered him. And suddenly I felt I might yet be home again.

At the hotel the taxicab driver palmed a dollar of my change, and I *knew* I was home again. I laughed as I registered at the desk. Laughed for the first time since the boy robbed me a month ago.

I stand in front of a bar in the French Quarter. The band inside plays "Muskrat Ramble" and the liquid, honey-sweet music like making love with joy rolls over me and brings with it a sudden burst of happiness rising inside, a joy unknown for years, like a celibate suddenly feeling the warm-sucking wetness of a woman's lips opening his mouth, slipping, sliding down his flesh, a warmth flowing over his skin, his arms, his legs, his chest, all the joy of New Orleans, the French Quarter, the Storyville of my father's generation when jazz was created.

Joy washes over me and I am laughing, for the notes ring into my mind and I remember listening to Muggsy Spanier in Chicago when I was a boy, just after I was wounded, and with him Sidney Bechet, whom I first heard in the Quarter, then later in Chicago at the old Blue Note, before he emigrated to Paris. Bechet, for me, true to his art—never compromising it as a showman the way Louis Armstrong did—always plumbing his soprano saxophone for the pain and the joy of life.

Joy washes over me in a great sheet.

The band shifts to "Bye, Bye, Blackbird."

My eyes squirt with sudden and totally unexpected tears, for this was Dad's favorite song, the one he hummed as we drove south, his big hands taut upon the steering wheel, his foot hard upon the accelerator, his lips sucking wetly on his unlit cigar.

I wander into the bar and order a martini.

Five hours and five martinis later (they were watered of course!) I am as high and as happy as I have been in years. Joy expands in my chest like the embrace I needed, for it takes me back and back and back to the old songs, the drunken songs, the gay songs, back to the Quarter, the old Love-for-Sale Quarter, when in the forties the pimps were as thick as crayfish crawling over a Louisiana road, the whores selling their wares on the street. Back to the years of my youth, before the wounding, back to the time when my years were not rimmed by violence, when Dad's rifle was just a rifle, not a symbol of all weapons to be feared. Back to those days. Staring at this lovely young blonde in the corner with big tits unfettered by a brassiere; her eyes meet mine and, for a moment, a brilliant moment, I forget my failures, forget my divorce, forget Dad's death, wondering if maybe, just maybe, there is not a future for me again, not even wanting to pick her up but only sit and stare. Then I leave, drunk with delight.

I slept that night.
I did not dream.

Dark roast coffee with chicory and beignets! Black coffee, a little bitter: "Black as night, sweet as faith, hot as hell!" The beignets fluffy as a summer cloud.

How many times have I sat here at the French Market? The round tables, iron chairs, tourists with cameras and postcards. Jackson Square, where Great-grandma Watson had an apartment in the Pontalba buildings; the cathedral where Dad and his brothers dumped ink into the holy water on Sunday mornings just before mass; a few blocks away, the seaman's bethel that Grandma Watson ran. I had sat here with my uncles and my cousins, had breakfast in the market café behind me at seven in the morning, after drinking all night in the Quarter.

I had sat here with Dad in 1962 when mother was dying at Ochsner's Hospital from cancer, lying in pain for eighty days and nights, at the end panting for air like a fish out of water, just before her death, her hair coming out in great gobs from her chemotherapy, her breasts sliced away by the surgeon, then her lung and ribs removed, cancer now in her brain. Her brown eyes, her soft brown eyes unseeing, my mother, my mother, my mother. Dad and I would flee from the hospital to the Quarter, eat at Antoine's or Galatoire's or the Commander's Palace, then come to the French Market and have coffee as we tried to laugh. As she sucked in air in great gasps, her eyes so liquid soft like the deer Dad had once killed.

We drank in the Quarter and, on Sunday afternoon, when I had to go back to New England, Dad would take me to the airport and we would have another martini and another and another, until I boarded the airplane. I would see him there as I left him—alone, driving back to the hospital where they had sliced off her breasts, those soft round globes on which I had nestled. Another killing ground.

She died in great pain in her chemotherapy, died, damn it, blind, desperately sucking in air, died in New Orleans where it all began, lying on her back in that hospital, her lovely hair gone, her hands wasted, this, my mother, this the mother of the letters and her love, this my mother, the one I have lost.

I've come back to the hotel room to lie down. I feel terribly upset. My stomach jerks a little. I'm sweating.

My only companion in this room is Dad's rifle. I stare at its leather case and imagine the blue-steel barrel lying within.

I remember the madmen of the day, that boy at the University of Texas who climbed the tower and killed a dozen people before he was killed himself. Is this why I brought this rifle south? Is there some unknown and unspeakable violence buried deep within me that, now, at last, with Dad's death, I must release?

Why does his rifle attract me so? Why do I need to fire it?

There's a rifle range listed in the yellow pages, out by Airline Highway. I've called them up. I must fire that weapon. I can't explain it. Maybe it's my ownership. Maybe being back here close to Dad. Maybe all the memories. . . . The steel-barreled rifle is contained deep within my mind's soul. Has it always been?

Has the image of Dad's rifle always been the controlling force of my life, unknown to my conscious mind but determining who I really am and all that I have become? Its meaning has magnified in intensity in the past few days, especially since I was robbed, especially since I reached New Orleans. Is it that my conscious mind, the protection of so many years, is being worn down by my closeness to the past? These memories? My father? Mother? These women? Is it my father's truth with which I must finally deal?

I cannot believe it. Here on the edge of this city of six hundred thousand people, a rifle range has been erected. Firing ranges of 100, 200, 300, 500 yards for rifles; 50, 100, 200 feet for pistols. There's a great warehouse of guns and rifles through which the customer must walk on the way to the range. Every weapon I've ever heard of in my life is here. Every make. Every caliber—and every shape and age and color of human being buying them. (No racial prejudice in the sale of weapons!) Boys—at least they look young to me, like the boy who robbed me. Grandfathers leaning on their canes and grandmothers in Mother Hubbards. Sleek and sexy women; are they whores buying pistols of love? Vietnamese testing .32s and .38s as if they were buying milk or bread. Men in polyester, men in tweed, men in denim. Skins black and yellow and brown and red and white. My God! Has the whole world turned into a gun?

No one cares that I carry a .30-caliber Winchester rifle in its leather case.

At the entrance to the range I pay $37.50 for fifty shells and the use of the 100-yard range. (I think I'd better start at a short distance. The last time I fired a rifle was the day I was wounded in 1944.)

The man behind the counter is not just fat, he is obscenely fat. He wears a dirty T-shirt, stained under the armpits. His blue denim pants almost fall from under his gross belly. A tear in the shirt exposes the black hair just above his navel.

He motions through the glass door to the range with a bored expression. The rumble of the firing is intense. It rocks and roars. He points to the earplugs he has given me. I put them on. He walks ahead. I follow him to a firing station, blocked from those on either side by wooden frames. He points downrange. Ten—he raises the fingers of both hands—ten targets and fifteen minutes for my fifty shells.

He disappears.

I slam open the bolt. My fingers tremble.

One, two, three, four, five shells shoved into the magazine. As if I had never stopped firing, it all comes back so quickly. Slam home the bolt, first shell in the chamber. Half twist to the leather sling. Lift the rifle butt to the meaty part of my shoulder, not on the collarbone. Take a deep breath. Let it out. Half breath. Hold the needle of the sight just below the target. Squeeze the trigger gently, like caressing a woman's hard, extended nipple. Steady the sight. Hold it at the bull's-eye. Steady. Steady. Steady. Squeeze. WHAM! The rifle slams against my shoulder with the never-to-be-forgotten jolt, driving my shoulder back, the end of the rifle jerking up, smelling the just-remembered acrid perfume of gunsmoke drifting by my nose.

"Ten o'clock," a bored voice calls. "Missed the ring, but on the paper."

I stare downrange through the small spotting telescope provided for each shooter. The target is torn with the mark of the bullet as it just ticked the lefthand edge, above the center.

I change the clicks on the sight, then suddenly and unexpectedly fire the four remaining shells as fast as I can. As if I had to explode them from the barrel now that I had fired the rifle.

Then I relax and slowly and carefully proceed to fire the remaining forty-five shells.

I stand on the balcony of the hotel and stare down at dark faces sliding by on the sidewalk below. Hear, once more, soft voices slipping into the night. Much of my anger is gone.

I had to fire Dad's rifle this afternoon. Is it such rage that leads to mass murders? Such confusion, loss, uncertainty, feelings of guilt and loneliness? Having been so badly wounded myself, I could never injure another in that way. Yet I, in my confusion and in my rage, have known that desire. Possession of this rifle, the opportunity to fire it, released much of that terrible tension. Repressed rage like this must be the source of the violence in our nation.

Was there no answer, I wondered, as I left the hotel and strutted down the streets of the Quarter, hearing music rise from striptease joints where women, the children of poor whites, swung their bare bottoms to the raucous strains of rock and roll. Was there no answer?

I wanted to weep as a young girl, not more than fifteen, strolled by me and whispered: "Suck your cock for twenty dollars, mister? In the alley there?"

Was there no answer to our violence and our rage?

There was only the music like liquid joy as I passed the bar where I had sat the night before. Music made from the suffering of the alien black and the haunted beauty of the painted whore.

CHAPTER 9

THE SEARCH FOR TENDERNESS

> *For now we see through a glass, darkly:*
> *but then face to face . . .*
> —*1 Cor. 13:12*

In a rented car, I head south, down the road of my ancestors. Now it is my father I pursue as I drive old Route 90, past forts that defended the entrance to Lake Pontchartrain in the War of 1812, forts still collapsed into ruins, not yet historic monuments plasticized and romanticized by rules from Washington but forts I remembered from childhood when we landed at old Fort Morgan on Mobile Bay and Dad and I and my uncles and my cousins wandered through those battered walls, watching for rattlesnakes, opening creaky cell doors, finding old musket balls on dirt cracked floors, hiding, terrified, in those darkened cells, touching then for a moment the real past, not yet perverted by our modern image of what the past should be.

Yes, it is my father I pursue on this, the last leg of my journey. It is he I must understand to escape these strange days of my defeat. It is the meaning of the rifle he left to me as my inheritance that, finally, I must penetrate.

But how does one find one's real father, locate the true man in all those misty memories, the man before the father, the one who made the father? How do I find my real father, separate him from all he was supposed to be? How do I touch those generations of fathers? How do I pierce the hate and love and pain and the loss of what was, yet perhaps had never been, perhaps could never be?

FATHER? I cry as I ride these dusty roads which once took him north.

DAD?

And seem to hear his answering hymn, sung in saffron southern dusk: *You come on, Eddie. Come on in now, son. It's dark out there. You might get hurt.*

My father, my father, my father, the one I have lost, the father who became my enemy after I was wounded, the father before I took his rifle as my own, the father of tenderness, holding me high in the air, spinning me around the room, the father who wrote me letters of love after I was wounded, who took me on all those trips, who met with my psychiatrist, who carefully left me money to help pay for my kids' tuition when he died. Yes, it is the tenderness so lost in my life today that I seek, like water from a crystal spring. Tenderness of my peers in military hospitals, of my friends at the University of Chicago, tenderness of my many mothers, aunts, grandmothers *their voices, their sweet sweet voices* tenderness of my wife when first we met, tenderness now alive only in the vaults of memory. Tenderness, a value derided in the killing grounds of Cambridge and Washington in which I live, tenderness I so desperately need if I am to survive. Tenderness I reach for as I drive down these roads of my past, routes we followed when we took my mother to the hospital for her final stay, from New Orleans toward Mobile through Ocean Springs where Dad retired, unable to stop and see his home now owned by a stranger. Through Moss Point and Bayou la Batre and Coden, through all the towns of memory, toward the cemetery where he and my mother are buried, the road I finally must drive to its conclusion, the rifle in its leather case at my side.

I have visited this cemetery so many times: when Mom and Dad picked out the grave, before there was a stone, before my mother was buried here, before Dad's funeral. A small stream runs not far from the grave. The afternoon sun is warm. I close my eyes.

I think of my parents' pain and suffering, their love and hope for me. My mother's voice: Did I sleep without fear? Was I warm at night? Had I learned my catechism? Did I say my prayers? My father's voice reeling off the old stories about his relatives:

> *Once when I was a boy I watched my Cousin Bubba. Warn't certain what he was doing but it sure were right strange. Had a long thin tube in his hand and was holding it high in the air, sucking on it at one end.*
>
> *"Whatcha doing, Bubba?" I asked.*
>
> *"Whatcha think I'm doing?" he answered. "I'm sucking on this tube so young farts like you can ask me what I'm doing."*
>
> *"That's not what you're doing," I answered. "Tell me, Bubba. Whatcha really doing?"*
>
> *He got a right crafty look on his face. Stared over his shoulder to make sure nobody was listening. Stepped right close to me. "There's gold in the air," says he.*
>
> *"Gold?" I questioned.*
>
> *"Yeap, real gold," he says. "Blows here from Californy. Read about it in the newspaper. When they mine gold out there some of it blows into the air. Got to come east, don't it? Prevailing wind, ain't it? That's why I got this long tube. I suck down the air into this." He pulled out a filter, a filter the size of a damn cigar. "Pretty soon this filter's gonna be full of gold."*

I sit by the grave and remember and I think of them and of Lydia Tiffany and Grandma Green and Grandma Watson and all those aunts and uncles who came briefly together for the funeral but who have already disappeared and I wonder, what happened to them? What happened to all of us? How did my generation fail so badly?

Yes: failed the dream, the land, the family and the flesh in these five decades of my discontent.

The dream most of all: *a bright illusion from my populist forebears that out of violence we could create a society of splendid peace and justice.* . . . Fought for on the barren-brown fields of Spain, through the hedgerows of France and Germany's pine forests. An illusion held for a few brief moments after the war, betrayed in that bitter struggle between communism and democracy, the explosion of weapons technology, our fear of atomic annihilation, the assassination of Martin Luther King.

The land as well: *the bay spread out from the gumbo-muddy shore in soft green surges and schools of specks sped in choreographed unison through the clear salt water.* . . . Now neither fish nor oysters nor shrimp remain, only slicks of oil and great steel monsters, their mechanical cry drowning the voice of the sibilant sea.

And failed my family and our flesh: *the ancient brooding flesh from which I came, those great gatherings on humid Sunday afternoons beneath the moss-laden live oaks when mothers, grandmothers, aunts, uncles, kissing cousins and cousins once removed descended from the eroded fields and red-gullied farms upstate, bringing memories of days when Ol' Jack rode through the valley and Marse Robert swung up the heights of Gettysburg.* . . . Humid Sundays ending now with only a maiden aunt and a distant cousin still alive, silent in their rocking chairs on that great and empty porch. And failed our contemporary family as well, for who of us has not been divorced or separated, betrayed a friend on our rise to power, lost our love in those years of pain? Our early innocence, when our secure hearts reached beyond themselves in trust and gentleness, now only a hymn to our current desolation.

As a child, my greatest family joys came during summers on the Gulf Coast. We crabbed and fished in the Mississippi Sound every summer during the 1930s. No matter how poor we were after Dad went bankrupt in 1932, he always got us back to Bayou la Batre and Coden for a vacation in August.

Those were the days of the great family reunions. Relatives from Texas, Louisiana, Mississippi, Alabama. The summer cottage always thronged with people. God knows they all talked at the same time, but Dad's voice overwhelmed theirs.

In the early mornings, though, he always managed to spend time with me. We would rise before dawn, sneak out into the kitchen where he would have coffee heating in the old drip pot (one I still own). Dad would fry bacon and eggs, an apron covering his big belly. Neither of us talked as we forced sleep from our eyes.

We walked out into the dawn, early morning air just stirring, the last star still bright on the horizon. We trudged down the long wharf to the motorboat anchored by the reef of oyster shells. We pushed out into the silent sea.

Dad swore as he started the one-lung motor. For an hour, perhaps more, we put-putted toward the islands. I lay forward on the bow, staring down at the translucent water.

My uncles and cousins slept.

With the sun the joshing began. Who would catch the biggest fish? *Spit on the hook, boy. Remember when Watty fell over? Naw, he didn't fall over. Been drinking too much. Why, man, you know Watty done quit drinking, don't you?*

After we anchored we might sit for hours, waiting for a school of speckled or white trout to flash beneath the keel. In the meantime we caught croakers: they grunted when we took them from the hook.

Dad once caught a stingaree, three feet across its lightly mottled back. He fought it for over fifteen minutes. It finally sloshed to the surface, ugly protruding eyes rolling at us. Its bonelike tail lashed the water until it rolled belly up, flesh obscenely white under slowly moving batlike wings.

Dad cut the line to let it go.

"Gimme that gun, boy," Dad commanded.

He always carried a .410 sawed-off shotgun on the boat. Its barrel was silvered, about eighteen inches long, its handle curved like a pistol's. He lifted it, held it straight before him, dropped the barrel toward the stingaree with practiced skill.

"KROOMP!"

Blood exploded from the stingaree's belly. The fish turned and twisted in dying agony.

"Never liked those damn things," Dad grunted, breaking the barrel and ejecting the shell. He handed the gun to me. "Put it away, boy."

And we stared at our bobbers again.

Long days. Rolling days. Thunderheads rising over the sea at ten or eleven in the morning, towers of white against the fiercely blue sky, sometimes deep black at the horizon. Once waterspouts lifted their heads like twisting snakes between the clouds and the water. Calm before the storm. Elysian fields before the war.

We stared at our bobbers, occasionally replacing the shrimp we used for bait, threading the hook through its belly.

Dad was a magician and I his best audience.

The most entrancing times with Dad were during the Christmas holidays in Chicago and La Grange. I wonder if many people in the world ever experienced that magical holiday as we did.

Dad would start buying presents immediately after Thanksgiving. He rushed up the stairs when he came home, a happy smile on his face, his latest gift hidden under his overcoat as he searched for a place to hide it. His buying and hiding of presents went on and on and on and on.

I was wild with impatience. Who wouldn't be?

The excitement of gifts and Santa Claus and knowing relatives would soon arrive. Seeing the big boxes of seafood shipped from the South stacked in great piles in the back yard where they would stay frozen: gallons of oysters and shrimp and red snapper throats and redfish. Wild turkey shipped from Texas along with a venison leg. Smoked hams from Virginia. The house throbbed with anticipation. The gifts stacked three feet high and five feet wide under the tree, encircling its base, a pile of white- and red- and green-wrapped packages reaching toward the ornaments we had used ever since I could remember. On Christmas morning, Dad pranced around the gifts crying in his joyous voice, "Christmas gift. Christmas gift."

A time of magic and miracles.

A time that started to die before I was born. A time that died finally and irrevocably after World War II.

World War I had really started that erosion. Dad's years as a pilot filled him with ambition to become a wealthy man. His brother went to France, met his wife-to-be there, a marriage that ended in a divorce, the first in our large family.

The Depression of the 1930s, ironically, reinforced the strength of our family. Though separated by thousands of miles, as far apart as Chicago and Texas, the family was all we had. There was little government aid. Houses were immediately gobbled up by banks when mortgage payments fell behind. If one lost one's job, without family support one lost everything. That simple. Dad and his brothers, my mother and her sisters somehow kept each other going. When Dad was in the hospital in 1932, his bills were paid by family members. When Dad started making money again in the late 1930s, my mother sent a check each month to my grandmother. That helped prevent the loss of the family farm.

Families still cared for their members. The love and support of brother for brother, sister for sister, child for parent bridged poverty and separation.

Yet, even so, the erosion of that great family continued.

Pleasures were no longer defined by simple exchanges between friends and relatives. Entertainment stopped being formed around storytelling, singing, fiddle and banjo playing, people with people creating their own forms of joy. Radio and movies brought a new kind of magic into daily life, denying the easy familiarity of human contact, replacing it with the fantasies and illusions of commercialized programs. The automobile opened new vistas, most of all the opportunity for unbridled sexual experience.

These social changes set the framework for Dad's career. He first learned his skills at making money in the twenties, the decade following World War I. Selling paint in all those small southern towns in Mississippi, Louisiana and Texas helped him learn his seductive charm and power.

No one ever understood how Dad really ran his business after he opened his yarn brokerage in Chicago in the 1930s. He kept his filing system in his head and on the backs of crumpled old envelopes he carried in his pocket. He lived on the telephone.

He knew the secret of his time. Paper and procedures were for those afraid of life; the trick was to subvert all regulations in order to reach success. Human beings always made decisions, often violating rules. Go straight to the decision maker.

"Eddie," he once told me, "don't ever worry about money. It's a commodity like everything else. Banks just sell it. Interest is their price. What you got to know, boy: bankers are suckers for the big story, not the small." That knowledge had helped him find a job at the bottom of the Depression.

In 1932 he went bankrupt. Lost his paint store, our house, everything. All that kept him and my mother going was the help he had from his employed brothers and the food my grandmother sometimes shipped us. By 1933 the pressure became so great that he collapsed and was taken from our home to the hospital in an ambulance.

He suffered from a purported case of massive arthritis. "My joints don't work right anymore, Eddie."

Today he would have been diagnosed as having had a massive nervous breakdown.

He was in the hospital for a month, then at home for three. One day he suddenly got out of bed, put on his best suit, went down to the local bank, which had lent him the money to start his store, and talked the banker into a drawing account of seventy-five dollars a month. Out of some unknown place deep in his heart he had decided that the future belonged to cotton, a commodity with which he had never worked. He was convinced that soon there would be a great demand for it and that that demand would center in Chicago, a place he had lived for a few months before he enlisted in the Air Service in 1918.

Impossible? Crazy? But it worked.

We moved to Chicago in the worst of the Depression, October 1933. Lived on a case of tomatoes for two weeks. (I still hate the taste of them.) But, slowly, Dad began to make it.

Letters from 1935 and 1936 indicate that buyers were turning from their former sources of supply to buy their cotton threads from Mr. Wood ("Watson," as he was known in business) and the mills that used him as broker.

Audacity. Always audacity.

In the late 1930s Dad was audited by the Internal Revenue Service. The questions—rare in those days—must have been extremely serious, as the letter from the IRS requested that Dad bring his lawyer and his accountant to a meeting with the auditor.

He did so.

He told me later that the IRS auditor was a woman, a washed-out blonde in her late thirties or early forties.

"Mr. Wood," she began without any preliminaries, "we have some most serious problems with your return. Before we go into them, however, there is one small but important point I wish to get clear. You claim in December of last year that you took two people out to dinner at the Palmer House and spent thirty-seven dollars and fifty cents for dinner. [The equivalent of $225 today.] Even though it was the Palmer House, you know nobody can spend that much for food, Mr. Wood. Nobody."

Dad said he looked at her for a long, long time, searching

for the greed in her heart. His lawyer and his accountant stared at him, waiting for him to speak.

"Young lady," Dad finally spoke. "I *did* spend that much money for dinner. I *can* spend that much money for dinner. I *will* spend that much money for dinner. And I'll pick you up at six o'clock tonight to prove it."

She went to dinner with him. And he won his audit. Scot-free.

Audacity. Always audacity.

Magic. Always magic.

He always kept his marvelous spirit and bravado, his willingness to undertake risks. By the late 1930s and early 1940s he was coming home from work by three or four o'clock in the afternoon. He would bother my mother a little, go out for coffee with friends, sing a song, watch me and my high school friends play basketball and, when we were older, poker. He made friends with anyone.

Yet, with the years, his magic slowly died. Died, I think now, because he lost his ability to utilize his feminine instincts, his marvelous intuitive reach into the souls of others. The conflict between, on one side, his ruthless search for power and money, and on the other side, his charm and intensely emotional caring, finally destroyed who he really was.

By the time he died, all that seemed to matter to him were the things he owned.

It happened to all men of his generation. They beat the Depression. Crafted the victory that won World War II. Acts of giants.

Think of them: Roosevelt, Marshall, Churchill. They lived out their lives on killing grounds. In winning on those grounds, using any means of war, including the bombing of innocent civilians, in building those great systems of governments and armadas centered on the goal of destroying the enemy, they lost their capacity for compassion.

Their power came simply from being Anglo-Saxon males born at the beginning of the twentieth century. Surely the best opportunities always came to such men, whether American, English, Australian, New Zealanders, Northern Europeans or Canadians. Simply put, the world's population increased by over 2 billion in their lifetime. At Dad's birth, just after 1890, there were only 63 million Americans; in 1950, 150 million; by 1972, at his death, over 200 million. These persons all required goods and services and, by God!, Dad and his peers would provide them.

Dad knew from his youth what power meant.

He made the declamation at his high school graduation on June 1, 1911, at seventeen years of age. His subject: "The Supremacy of the Anglo-Saxon Race." In all those papers stacked in his garage after his death, I found what I believe to be a rough copy of that speech. Written in his sprawling hand, crossed out, worked over, it was obviously an event of supreme importance in his youth.

I imagine him standing on a platform in that humid Mississippi weather, slim, debonair, his hands thrusting into the air as he spoke, singing his hymn to freedom:

> *This is our Anglo-Saxon heritage. Passed to us by brave men who died for their faith and wisdom, who brought freedom to our shores.*
>
> *Many of them—the best of them, the most important, the bravest—came directly to the South, most of all to the great state of Virginia, birthplace of the nation, bringing with them the Anglo-Saxon tradition . . . Freedom. Aye! Sweet freedom.*

[Here, I imagine rebel yells interrupting his words.]

> *No foreign king or authority telling us what to do.*
>
> *No foreign king or authority collecting taxes.*

> *No foreign king or authority daring to*
> *enter our homes.*
> *Freedom . . . brought to our nation by men*
> *willing to die for this belief, the Anglo-Saxon*
> *heritage passed on to us.*
> *Freedom!*
> *Freedom!*
> *Freedom!*

The wisdom of his era was pressed into his genes: an Anglo-Saxon male was free to do as he wished with his home, his property, his peasants—and, of course, his women!

Dad and his peers founded and protected those great systems which preserved that freedom, those killing grounds in which he finally lost his magic and his tenderness. The rifle I carry with me comes from those systems, not from his inherent tenderness.

This rifle I carry, loaded, into the South with me, masks all memories of his caress and love, that caring he gave me as a child. It denies the memory of my mother as well—those memories of the voices of my many mothers so destroyed after the war in the bitter struggles among my mother, father and me, memories lost after the war and my wounding, the special world I shared with the women of my family, places free of killing grounds. Such a special world we shared, their soft voices pressed deep into southern evening dusk, sibilant sigh of sea surf woven into their songs, their caring, their love for me *mothers, grandmothers, aunts, cousins, kissing cousins once removed* a phalanx of love and female flesh protecting me from the darkness of the night. My father's caress long before the rifle, my mother's love long before our pain. I long for them, grope for them, blindfolded, in this everlasting game of life and death.

I am lucky for I can still hear their voices in all the letters my father left me, in those photographs which form the

kaleidoscope of my many mothers, the hundreds of letters my
mother wrote me—best of all the one that still brings tears to
my eyes, the one full of her compassion, written the day she
learned I was wounded:

> La Grange, Illinois
> September 26, 1944
>
> *Dearest Eddie,*
>
> *You know how my heart goes out to you
> now. Everything in me cries out to help you!
> How I wish you were not so far away but when
> I think it could be the South Pacific instead of
> England I am glad that you are because you can
> get home quicker from there.*
>
> *Two letters came yesterday, the one dic-
> tated by you and the other from the Red Cross
> and the Red Cross lady who wrote your letter.*
>
> *We are so deeply concerned about your
> injuries and your arm. Thank goodness the
> head injury is no worse but I am sure it is bad
> too. I surely hope that the buttock injury is not
> very deep and I do so hope you have been given
> something to keep you from suffering. What
> can you tell us about where you were when it
> happened? How long were you in France be-
> fore they brought you to England?*
>
> *I trust that help came to you as soon as you
> were hurt, as you couldn't do much to help
> yourself with a bad arm and injured the way you
> were. Let us know all of this when you can write.*
>
> *Send us your address in the hospital as
> soon as you can. In this way our mail will reach
> you quicker, I know.*
>
> *We are going to try and get a cable through
> to you, as we do so want you to know our
> thoughts and our prayers are with you. This
> you already know I am sure.*

> *Try to get a letter written to us at least
> once a week, if you can. Maybe it will not be so
> long before you can write.*
>
> *Wish they would send you back to the
> States to recuperate. I want you to promise to
> stay there and take care of yourself.*
>
> *All my love and kisses,*
>
> > *Devotedly,*
> > *Mom*

That letter, and all her other letters written to me in the war, open my memory to the years when my mother and I were so close before that bloody wounding. When Dad moved us to Chicago in 1933, after his bankruptcy, we left the middle-class neighborhood of Meyers Park, outside of Charlotte, North Carolina (where Dad spun me around in the living room after the air circus), for a totally different situation on Chicago's South Side.

Dad had lived at 6730 S. Lowe in 1917 and 1918 after he graduated from college, boarding with his cousins while he worked as a clerk in the city. At that time it had been a most respectable middle-class neighborhood of single-family homes and a few walk-up apartments. But by the 1930s the northern European immigrants had moved farther south, replaced by Polish descendents, largely Catholic—to my mother's horror.

We rented the second story of a two-apartment flat at 6921 S. Lowe and, within a year, moved to 6742 S. Lowe, a cheaper place. (Dad's income continued its decline.)

If, for me, the move north was a disaster, for my mother it must have been a cataclysm. I could find no pals in school, my southern accent mocked by tough little boys who beat me up every day as I walked home. The building, a three-story, monolithic brick structure, loomed over the dirt playground like a medieval fortress. I lived in absolute terror for those two years.

My mother experienced an isolation just as grim. No friends for either of us. A strange and terrible climate—the cold in winter, the bitter wind that froze our bones. Once Mother fell on the ice, walking through the underpass beneath the railroad just behind our flat; it took her over forty-five minutes to finally stagger up the hill.

Dad, of course, was never home. He was always on the road, trying to establish his business. My mother and I became so sweetly close. Friends, companions. I suspect that, with my father gone so much, I became for her her only confidant. She read to me, her dear voice always protecting me from the terror outside our home.

She waited for me at the corner by our flat at 3:30 PM, after I walked from school. We went to movie matinees together, double features costing a dime. She took me to the library, made sure I read the books she took out for me.

In our isolation, she supported me, warmed me, held me.

And I probably gave her just as much.

Later, as Dad made more money, she was the force behind our moves. First, farther out on Chicago's South Side, then to La Grange—motivated always, I am sure, by her desire that I be enrolled in the best school systems. She took magazines like *The Saturday Review of Literature*, joined the Book of the Month Club. We went to plays in the Loop. She began to paint, a fine pastel I still own one of her best works. She loved working with her hands and decorated our home with her crafts. She cooked the most delicious food. She was the force that made our home livable in the Great Depression when a whole society collapsed, made a retreat free from killing grounds for my father and me.

Oh, I remember now her love and her letters, the voices of so many mothers embracing me, holding me, caressing me, oh, how I long to hear them once more, now that they are dead. Why, *why*, when she was alive, had I rejected Mother so fiercely, seared her with my rage and anger?

Yet, how else could I defend myself? In some way I shall never understand, my wound linked us. Her love and her caring for me were so strong, my need for her so great, we came too close. And, for a time, I could relate to no other woman but her and in that relation we both stumbled into some nightmare that haunted both of us.

In 1955 Mother had a double mastectomy, in 1961 a lung and some ribs were removed, in 1962 the cancer metastasized into her brain. She began chemotherapy but died that June, and I held her hand while she panted like a goddamn fish and died, her eyes glazed, her gorgeous brown hair so thin and wispy.

In those years I turned toward power, beginning my studies at MIT, fleeing, fleeing, fleeing down those cold corridors, so far out of touch with myself as I sought to emulate my father, his success with money and women.

I weep inside myself for all the pain I caused.

Yet I was mad. Mad from all those years of suppressing my desires. Mother would not let me go. WOULD NOT LET ME GO, GODDAMNIT! My wound still linked us. I pulled and tugged and yanked as if I could escape only by cutting her from my life. Did her cancer begin then, when I rejected her so brutally, refusing to see her for five years?

In some way I could not understand, did my acts depress her so deeply she turned upon herself?

I do not know.

For a time I did seek her destruction. To be free, I treated her with great barbarity.

What was I to do?

SHE WOULD NOT LET ME GO.

I fear I yanked the flesh from her bones in leaving.

Her love for me killed her, my love for her almost destroyed me. More than any act of my life, I regret the pain I gave her.

I sit by the edge of their grave and think of all my failures, of all their failures, of those bodies locked deep within the ground. I think and I remember and I wonder about myself. What have I done with my life? Have I not done as Dad did? Have I not lived in the corridors of power, seeking influence, control, sex—what a man is supposed to have? Oh, yes, surface goals of social justice—but, at the bottom of my heart:

My writing? No more. Art? No more. God? No more. Nature? No more. I have denied those values I lived by in rural Connecticut in the fifties.

Yes, I sit by this grave and think of all those failures, those myths and migrations, those letters of my mothers, rifles of my fathers, Dad's sale of the Blandford farm, think of all these things, of all we have become, violence and killing grounds, the rifle I still carry with me hidden in its leather case on the seat of the rented car. I think on all these things and, instantly, completely and totally I know why I have brought this rifle with me, and I begin to weep. I weep hot tears from my open eyes, wet my cheeks in great salt sheets and I reach up and I want to scream at the arch of the sky, scream a mighty yell of rebellion and rage and if I had that rifle in my hands I would use it on myself after blowing up the world for there is no fairness or justice but only one long road of suffering and pain which reaches from one grave to another and I have rejected my father and my mother in the arrogance of my youth and the crush of my wound and we had never talked since I was a boy. I weep and I weep and I weep until my sobs slowly cease.

I reach over and caress the gravestone before I leave, and wish that I could kiss those old bodies resting in the hollowed soil below.

CHAPTER 10

GIVING UP THE RIFLE

> *When I was a child, I spake as a child, I understood as a child, I thought as a child: but when I became a man, I put away childish things.*
>
> —*1 Cor. 13:11*

I chartered a small sailboat last night, a twenty-seven-foot sloop. The owner questioned my ability to sail, but after half an hour I proved my skills.

Forty years have passed since I sailed these waters toward the Gulf islands. Still, my moves are automatic, all clumsiness forgotten as I complete the route of my father. Come about. Reach. Run. Jibe. Almost as if these years had never passed and now I am a child again. I imagine Dad below deck as he fries us grits and ham and eggs on our old gasoline stove. I shut my eyes as we round the tip of the island where we once moored.

I think of Dad and the life he led, the life most men lead in this, my country. I think of him as child and youth in that small and protected world, the bayou and its marshes, New Orleans, Storyville, the image of that house in the Berkshire Hills, the memory of Lydia, his grandmother, still pure and pristine in his heart. I think of the compassion he gave, caring for his parents, the love of his brothers, love for me, his loyalty to my mother as she died. I think of his tenderness and all it meant to me. I think of his years in the Air Service, of the terrible burdens he bore in the 1930s and '40s: depression, bankruptcy, war, my wounding, my rebellion.

Most of all I remember the magic and mystery of his love, the wonder he created for all of us. But as he aged, he lost his ingenuity in the bitter world of competition, rifles required for survival. He carried a rifle throughout his mature life, used it, used it well to accumulate those goods in that great house. Money, status, power, his inheritance to me. He was practically coronated as a king when he returned to Mississippi after selling the family farm in Blandford.

By then I hated him. He had made his wealth from the war in which I was wounded and, in some way I never understood, was implicated in my wounding, my torn flesh and blood. If I had not been wounded, if I had, instead, used his rifle, my inheritance, to kill and wound others, my life would have been so different. My relationship with my father would have been rooted in the companionship of the weapon instead of being ruptured by my bitter rage, the rage in which we lost each other, never to really talk as father and son in all our mature lives, never to share as fathers and sons should, each of us furiously alone, parted by the wound and my closeness to my mother.

We might have been friends instead of enemies.

Yet I *was* wounded in that war. I did turn to my mother instead of to Dad. I became a different being, no longer a boy, not yet a man, lost in the land of the wounded.

. . . But, even so, Dad's rifle still seduces me.

I stare at it in the cockpit beneath my feet, its blue-steel barrel, the crisp click of its precisely machined bolt, the ease with which the metal chamber receives its brass cartridge, melding of the walnut stock to hard steel, snap of leather sling supple from neat's-foot oil, blued butt plate opening to contain brass can of oil, round telescope sight with upright needle that settles lightly on the target's chest. *Take a deep breath. Let it out. Half breath. Steady. Caress the trigger like a woman's tit.* WHAM!!! The butt slams back against the shoulder and instantly, magically, the bullet explodes into flesh two hundred yards away, tumbles, tears, rips gristle and muscle and meat and artery, shreds bone and cartilage and nerve and vein as victim slams back into earth, consequences never seen on all those movies or on TV, blood that reeks of salty urine, feces suddenly passed, stink of fetid body matter, the frantic staccato of feet hammering on hollow earth, legs and arms twitching spasmodically, pallor of the skin, sudden passing of body gas mixed with blood, and fear, the awful GODAMIGHTY shouting fear *OH, SWEET JESUS, DON'T LET ME DIE. DIE. DIE. DIE. PLEASE. PLEASE. PLEASE I'LL DO ANYTHING. WON'T CUSS. WON'T SMOKE. WON'T DRINK. WON'T FUCK. WON'T JACK OFF ANYMORE* the bleat of animals after the hit, frantic twisting of the deer's head, clash of horns on rock, legs lashing out in final complaint.

Dad's rifle I have brought with me, my inheritance as an American man, this rifle and all the beliefs that accompany it, beliefs my father and his generation willed to me, the rifle always the ultimate reality beneath those shiny words of honor and of glory, this the reality my country really worships, presented on all those TV programs where Starsky and Hutch, Barnaby Jones, Rockford, Sonny and Rico blow 'em up with knife and gun. In all those movies I absorbed as a child where Bogey, Gary, Errol, John Wayne always win, slam a man in the mouth without breaking a knuckle, get shot and two days later are well, and there's ALWAYS a beautiful woman who supports their violence. Men who never lose, the heroes of American history: George Washington, Daniel Boone, Davy Crockett, Robert E. Lee, Stonewall Jackson, Buffalo Bill, Wyatt Earp, men whose word and universe were weapons. Shoot 'em up with guns like great penises that could explode in the vagina of the world. Guns like the one the boy shoved so hard in my belly. Guns, guns, guns, pistols that could put a hole in a man the size of a pencil and rifles that could put a hole in a man the size of a fist. Guns evolving into the massed slaughter of the Civil War and World War I and World War II and Korea and Vietnam, airplanes, bombers, napalm, infrared sights for killing at night as well as day, culminating in our final obscenity, atomic and hydrogen bombs . . .

Was this my real inheritance as an American male? Spend my life on killing grounds so as to defeat my enemies? Kill rather than admit that part of us longed to be like our mothers, soft and gentle, receive as well as take, give as well as demand? Was not this the fundamental male conflict, Dad's as well as mine?

I remember the magic he once possessed as I round up into the wind, the sea almost flat about me, the darkly green salten sea. Sails flap as I walk forward and wait for the boat's momentum to stop. I take the anchor in my hands, let it sink gently to the bottom of the sound ten feet below the keel. The boat sags back on the anchor. I play out the rope and let the anchor bite. I snub the line on the cleat. I stare to the east.

There is no longer an iron pipe. But I see a roiling on the surface of the water, a bubbling up from the bottom.

I swing the stern around with an oar, reach down, put my fingers into the water. It tastes sweet. By instinct I have found the artesian well of my childhood, after forty years.

I slide the rifle into the sun. On sudden impulse, I take some bullets, slam them into the chamber. Throw the rifle to my shoulder. Drop the sight on an oyster shell lying on the island's shore.

Steady. Full breath. Half breath. Caress the trigger.

WHAM!

The shell explodes into fragments.

KILLING GROUNDS. MOTHERFUCKING KILLING GROUNDS.

I fire at oyster shells again and again and again. The rifle bucks against my shoulder, hurts.

The boy who just robbed me.

The Jews the Nazis killed.

Slave laborers we liberated.

Men who assassinated two Kennedys and a King.

La femme scalpée with her clothes stripped, her shaven hair.

My work in Cambridge and in Washington.

Those TV shows that worship violence—rifles, shotguns, pistols, bazookas, tanks, bombers, machine guns, missiles, A-bombs, hydrogen bombs. We were the arsenal of the world, able to blow up its vagina. My nation had evolved into a military state in this century of war.

Trembling, I fire my last bullet.

The shore is littered with fragments of exploded oyster shells. Brass casings lie scattered over the deck. Sweat beads my brow though the day is cool.

I have hesitated an hour. I stare at Dad's rifle I hold so tightly in my hands.

We all hold a loaded rifle, I think, as I tighten my finger around the trigger. We all stand like animals, prepared to kill those who strike at us on the killing grounds of life.

I cannot keep this weapon any longer. I can never kill or wound again, not myself most of all.

I carry the rifle to the bow of the boat, almost stumbling over the coiled halyard.

Beneath me, the artesian well bubbles up through salt water. I lift the rifle and hold it over the bow. Can I, at last, give up the rifle, my father's legacy?

I hesitate.

I sweat.

Can I discover a life as deep as the everlasting sea where the self-discipline of compassion will wash the shores of my despair and set me free?

Since I entered the land of the wounded so many years ago, my whole life had trembled on the edge of suicide; at any moment I might have destroyed myself. Only my writing, those journals of so many years, only my children, requiring my stability, only those few years in Connecticut when I discovered art and nature and God, only these have kept me from my self-destruction.

All the rest?

Those years when I, like Dad, bowed to the legacy of the

rifle and its labyrinthine course? I had lost myself in power and its pursuit, become a being I loathed, deserting wife and children for trivial perks, just as Dad destroyed his tenderness once he used his rifle for survival.

Could I, at last, give it up, his legacy, find life's other meanings, so long denied? State that the most important contribution I can make to life is not power and its accumulation, not money, but the ability to care for another human being to the fullest depth of my heart (in fatherhood most of all) and not be washed away by female juices, flooded into nothingness? Care for women as events of grace and love, the vision of them watering my eyes with tears, the voices and letters of my many mothers alive again in spirit if not in flesh? Caress feminine bodies not as sexual objects in pornography as I had been taught, but, instead, love their thighs, their fluids, their breasts for what they are, the graceful body of another human being?

My fingers clench even tighter around the trigger. I hesitate. I sweat.

I have known the consequences of war, watched its tracery of wounds etched out upon my emotions and my flesh, known their repercussions, seen their impacts eat into my relations with my wife, shadow my love for my children, destroy my caring for my parents and theirs for me. The innocent suffer most in war: their suffering is carried on to their children, their children's children, on and on and on until all future generations are tainted by the pain of that inheritance, born of war.

Give up the rifle?

I must.

My fingers open.

The rifle tumbles down into the clear artesian water below me. The barrel glints and twists as it sinks deep into pure water, surrounded by the dark and murky sea *my father's hands heavy on the stock as he drew the rifle from its leather case.* The strap weaves in the gentle currents below.

We are all wounded by life, I think, the steel still

glimmering far below me. Some wounds we receive as children and youths: misconceived love of parents that seeks to force us into its image of their truth, warped genes of our inheritance that falsely brand our flesh and mind, wounds meshed into our fantasies during long warm nights, wounds from violence that shred our torn and screaming flesh. Other lesions we receive as adults, when friends betray us and lovers leave us. Age brings other wounds as well, as our children see in us what we once saw in our own parents and our bodies wither and wrinkle and we know, at last, that we will soon die with few of our dreams fulfilled.

Scar is piled on scar until we come to believe that the scars determine who we really are, cut into our once pure and pristine flesh with the scalpel of time. Our one task in life, our one hope, our one faith, is to reach deep beneath those scars, for far in our past, as deep as this artesian spring, lies our original self, our innocent soul, which defines our perfection and rises from clear and limpid wells into which we can hurl our anger and our despair and watch them absorbed by crystal-clear and eternal waters.

Is that not what I have done on this trip? Gone back and back and back into the past? Before MIT, Washington, Baltimore, Connecticut, University of Chicago, Charlotte, New Orleans, Springhill, Mobile, Moss Point, Ocean Springs, Bayou la Batre . . . back and back and back before I knew of killing grounds, before I used my father's rifle, back to the voices of my many mothers, hymns of childhood, my father's tenderness before he lost his magic, back and back and back and there is no time and the end is the beginning and the beginning is the end and I am in time and out of time and the sea hisses again at my side and the sun is hot upon my face with the old straw hat pulled down over my eyes, beams glaring on the bobber rising, falling with the waves. There is no time, no time, no time.

I hear Dad's voice at my side, no longer my enemy as he stares over the gunwale at speckled trout slashing at our shrimp, his belly bulging hard above his belt, a shout of joy on his lips. *You catch 'em, boy. You catch 'em, Eddie. We'll take 'em home to your momma for our supper.*

There is no time, and he and I are together again before the rifle, before he gave it to me as my legacy. I smile and listen once more to tales of his giant and magical days as he goes below to fix a pot of coffee.

And I know what I must do: cruise these waters for one last trip before I return north to my home.

PART V

LIFE WITHOUT THE RIFLE

CAPE COD
FRANCE

[1975–1983]
1984

CHAPTER 11

LIFE OUTSIDE KILLING GROUNDS

> *Glory be to God for dappled things—*
> *For skies of couple-colour as a brinded cow;*
> *For rose-moles all in stipple upon trout*
> *that swim;*
> *Fresh-firecoal chestnut-falls; finches' wings;*
> *Landscape plotted and pieced—fold, fallow,*
> *and plough;*
> *And áll trádes, their gear and tackle and*
> *trim.*
>
> *All things counter, original, spare, strange;*
> *Whatever is fickle, freckled (who knows how?)*
> *With swift, slow; sweet, sour; adazzle, dim;*
> *He fathers-forth whose beauty is past change:*
> *Praise him.*
>
> —Gerard Manley Hopkins, *"Pied Beauty"*

CAPE COD, 1984

I've worked all day as a gardener again. I cleaned a bed of pachysandra, planted some impatiens, the red-and-white variety, and edged the bed with a dark, sharp line of earth. Sometimes as I worked, I lifted my head and stared at the arching blue sky above me, pines black and green against

high-piled cumulus clouds. The sweet perfume of honey-
suckle softened the afternoon's heat and, at the end of the day,
I drove to Old Silver Beach in Falmouth (the parking fee stops
at four o'clock) and had a swim in the low surf of Buzzards
Bay before fixing myself a martini and drinking it in my back
yard, overlooking Cape Cod Canal.

It's a different way of life than those years in Washington
and Cambridge when I lived in killing grounds. I haven't been
to a meeting in years, trapped in plastic modules with artificial
air. Nor have I smoked a cigarette, read or (better yet!) written
a report, spent the night in a hotel room or felt so many
failures as a man.

From the moment I returned north after my cruise through
the Mississippi Sound, I knew I must leave the system of
killing grounds I had so long supported. No good could ever
come from societies based upon the rifle and its use. Since
dropping Dad's rifle into those artesian springs, I've once
again followed my deepest desires. I continued my career as
a city planner while the kids were in college to help pay their
tuition. But I hated every minute of it, knowing the work
destroyed me, but disciplining myself to that effort, essential
to their future. The moment I paid my youngest daughter's
final bill, I quit. Walked out. Left. Believing—no, knowing—
that the system in which I worked was a lie, no longer really
concerned with the protection of the land. The words were
mighty, magnificent, those reports I wrote; the promises were
of a life of beauty, those plans I made. But the deeds? Lowly,
serving the system's economic masters.

I returned to the life I had lived in Connecticut in the
1950s, the only model I had for life without the rifle. Art:
writing this book about killing grounds and keeping my
journals, what I wrote as a young man stronger now, rooted
in these years of struggle for maturity. Nature: living once
again in the out of doors, in this house I've rented just at the
edge of the Cape Cod Canal. Two bedrooms, natural pine

flooring and walls, as isolated in the winter as if I lived in northern Maine. After the first two years I ran out of money and started work as a gardener again. Each day, spring, summer and fall, I'm out of doors, an organic attachment to the earth, supple strength of my flesh. God: the God of these seasons, the God of their force, the God of compassion, the God of my mothers.

Once more I attend Quaker meeting, in Yarmouth, at the other end of the cape. The meeting house is a simple structure, warm with grained wood given its soft sheen by two hundred years of human caress each Sunday morning. When I sit in those ancient benches, I know my bottom is connected to the wooden pew, the pew to the floor, floor to joists, joists to sills, sills to earth, earth to roots, roots to branches, branches to leaves, leaves to air and water, rising toward the sky.

Art. Nature. God.

I moved to Cape Cod by accident—yet, on some deeper level, I was compelled by an unconscious instinct that took me back to the place where Thomas Lumbert first settled in 1637. The road he took from Scituate to Barnstable lies not a hundred yards from my house. From the canal and its smooth-sliding tidal water, I can imagine him, his oxen and wagon, lumbering out of another system, the puritanical repression of Boston, into his moment of freedom.

I've even found the cellar hole his grandson built in Truro. Sited on the rising bank of a hill in Lombard Hollow, south facing, I've sat there and felt I touched him through time. I found a rock in the cellar hole, with oyster-shell cement he must have made still bonded to it. I stroke it sometimes as I write: it links me directly to my rural past, especially through this natural life I lead.

When I wake in the morning I see ducks through my bedroom window. I watch the evergreens in their delicate ballet as the wind choreographs dancing branches. I hear the foghorn at the entrance to Cape Cod Bay calling the entrance to the canal.

I make no great impact upon society. Create no bold plans, write no ponderous position papers, fly no airplanes, produce no reports, spout no bureaucratic rules or regulations.

I live as simply as I can, totally out of the system of power and the need to possess it. I heat my house with wood, live in fifty-five- and sixty-degree temperature in winter. At the end of a day I have accomplished no splendid acts, impressed no one with my wit and wisdom. Instead, I have made a very tiny place—someone's garden—a little better. Cleaned out weeds. Planted some shrubs. Moved some mums. Raked some leaves.

And lifted my eyes to the heavens and felt myself intimate with the earth, just as much as the wild goose when it spreads its wings or stiffly sets its feet to land in driving wind, salt spray slashing its feathers ruffled slightly at the wing tip. Yes, as much a part of nature as the goose and the plants I water, knowing deep within myself nature's splendid beauty and its force of creation: waves curling on the beach, straight line of each comber rising, coiling, crashing, endless surge of green cut from depths of the sea; the undulating rise and fall of a kingfisher, interspersed with its sharp *scree* as it searches over the canal for food; the driven wildness of a school of minnows pursued by slashing bluefish, frantic splashes on the water's surface; the mystery of the canal with tidewater rushing at five or six knots, ceaseless hiss of power, declaring another force of God; the blue-beauty of a winter night when, temperature ten below zero, I walk the banks of the canal, white cakes of ice slipping over water's black surface while sea smoke dances on the darkly sliding sea, trembles in tiny puffs and whirls and feathery wisps, floating columns of mystery, fairies worshiping the magic of the night.

All this. Mine.

Not because I own it. Because I can't own it.

Because it is free.

In its freedom it is mine. And I am its.

And someday I will die and be merged into it and

perhaps I shall dance along the canal with the fog and stare back at this house and those who people it. And perhaps one day I shall be a goose and set my feet stiffly into the driving wind as it ruffles my feathers of white and black and gray.

On Sundays when I attend Quaker meeting, I sit in blessed silence and wait, my eyes closed, my hands open, knowing that, sooner or later, I will hear deep chords resonating within myself, in touch for an instant with time past, time present, time future . . .

Not that this is an easy life. Far from it. To give up power, oh, that is hard. Sometimes I am still lost without it, those three-piece suits, office suites, four-star meals and martinis. For the past winters, 1982 and 1983 and, now, this one of 1984, I've scarcely had enough money for heat. I've spent days in bed, blankets pulled over my head to stay warm.

There is something terribly depressing about being cold. It fills me with self-pity, the worst of American diseases. At fifty-nine years of age to be forced to search the railroad tracks for firewood, to plead with bill collectors to wait a few more days, to promise the oil company that I can pay for oil when I know I won't have the money, to borrow from friends and be humiliated when I can't pay on time.

I'm forced to sell family antiques in order to eat and stay warm. Selling them is like selling Dad himself. They ask me for a price for this clock and that painting. I can't put prices on things Dad owned. It's like putting prices on Dad's life.

Somehow, though, I understand that these years of grieving are essential to my discovery of a life outside of killing grounds.

By selling these goods, I slowly free myself from the need for things, seeing that things by their very nature keep us from who we really are. We must care for them, repair them, dust them, mortgage ourselves to pay for them, our essence determined by the quality and quantity of things we own. Dad owned so many things when he died, almost as if the things he owned were all that gave his life meaning, his magic and his mystery thoroughly destroyed.

Resigning from his consumer society is far more difficult than I had imagined. Yet there are so many benefits to this new life. I no longer deal with enemies each day. I'm free of them. I can listen to my own chords again. And most of all, once more, I grow closer to my children.

In those years of my double wounding, in those years when I sought to emulate Dad's power, I had no time to be the father I might have been. Those sixty- to eighty-hour work weeks, those airplane flights, those meetings, that drive for power, that terrible and uncontrollable force pounding inside (I would equal or beat Dad at his game!), all these obliterated fatherhood. MIT and Washington cared nothing for the demands of love. Parenting is meaningless in the drive for success, influence and material gain.

I ceded my rights to my children to my wife. But in the deepest corner of my heart I remembered. Oh, how I remembered: when my children were born and how my son's chin was squashed up against his face, soft flush of his skin, daughters' mews and swift movings, years when I cared for them in Connecticut, night feedings when my wife was nursing and needed sleep, their sucking mouths, holding them, burping them. Oh, I remembered the closeness between my wife and me as we built a home and lived in the natural world.

After the breakup of our marriage, I did what my father had once done for me. Took my kids on camping trips. Maine and the Adirondacks instead of the Gulf Coast. Backpacking to Mount Marcy and Mount Khatadin instead of canoe trips to Quetico. But the same freedom and love. We sat before campfires, laughed and joked. For me, it became the deep blood past, returning to Dad before our alienation, before I took his rifle for my own. Before the wound. Before he changed. Before I changed.

On some level I did not understand, I longed to recreate places free of killing grounds for my children as well as myself, resembling those places my mother, aunts, grandmothers had given me as a child. God knows it was not enough. Never enough to make up for those years of alienation. But I gave all I could with the fiercest love I could summon.

Yet, even here in a life outside of killing grounds, without enemies, why, when I lie down at night, do I still remember, with General MacArthur, "the crash of guns, the rattle of musketry, the strange, mournful mutter of the battlefield"? Why, when I walk by the high brick wall in Harvard Yard, do I cling to it, fearful of the hand grenade that might tumble over it, exploding at my feet? Why, in city streets, do I watch for snipers hidden in apartment windows? Why, on country walks, do I scrutinize terrain ahead, searching for cover, under uneasy threat of artillery fire? Why, sometimes in coffee shops and restaurants, when I hear the music of my youth, the big bands swinging to "I Walk Alone," "Begin the Beguine," "That Old Black Magic," do my eyes squirt with tears I cannot control, remembering so many losses in my life? Why does my head pulse with those fierce headaches, my fingers stay numb, my buttock and hip spasm with pain?

The war, that summer in France four decades ago, still throbs in flesh and heart, unforgotten, pressed into all I have become, though I have given up the rifle and changed my warlike ways. I still wonder at my manhood: Was I a coward on that day at the front? For Christ's sweet sake, why did those men treat me with such silence and contempt? Why did I fight so alone? Did I betray? Was I betrayed?

The news on radio and TV and in the papers continues its paean to war: out of our paranoia, our need for enemies, we arm ourselves, fight in dirty little wars—Central America, Africa, Afghanistan, Grenada, Lebanon and the Middle East—build mighty atomic armadas, even smear the sky with our weapons in Star Wars fantasy.

More boys of nineteen will be blown away.

Why? Why? Why? I ask myself. The consequences of that day still haunt me, call me back to France. I long to see those hills dropping down toward the Moselle River, hear the lonely mutter of the battlefield. I cannot complete my healing until I see the place of my wounding again. It beckons: forty years ago when, in a day, my entire life changed.

I've sold the rest of my father's antiques, except those I love the most.

The house is bare.

I'm leaving Cape Cod for France.

CHAPTER 12

RETURN TO FRANCE

"War was a fiend who stopped our clocks
Although we met him grim and gay."
                                        —Siegfried Sassoon
                                        Song-Books of the War

                    *   *   *

                                        Saint-Mihiel
                                        September 7, 1984

    Having discovered the place of my wound-
ing, forty years ago to the hour, I drive these
fields of combat all afternoon, filled with exult-
ant pride: Briey, Etain, Conflans, St. Marie aux
Chanes, swift memories of 1944. A wall there,
a hill, a group of houses where we thought the
Germans hid.
    Pride.
    Pride.
    Pride.
    More pride in that boy myself, my son, my
father than if he had been in combat for months.
Pride in him that he was a replacement; pride in
him that, without support, a friendly face, a
smile, a cheer, even a wink of recognition, he
stayed and did not run.

Aye! Pride.

He was no coward, doing it totally alone, a man already at nineteen.

In just these four days in France I have rediscovered why being a part of the liberation has meant so much to me. I came here to Saint-Mihiel totally by chance because I was so broke, because it held the youth hostel nearest to Metz and Verdun. I had forgotten that Saint-Mihiel was where our European commitment began in 1918, where my uncle fought. From September 12th to 16th that year, American forces liberated their first French town from the Germans. Twenty-six years later on September 2nd, 1944, the town was freed once more from the Germans by American troops. At the moment of liberation, the Nazis were preparing to kill twenty young men held as hostages.

We saved those young Frenchmen when we took the town.

The story repeats itself wherever I go, liberation an act of almost Godlike proportions to these French men and women who were freed from Nazi rule. From 1870 to 1918 and 1940 to 1944, eastern France was occupied by the Germans. Before that this whole area reeked of war—ruled by the Caesars, torn apart by Charlemagne and his sons, plundered in battles of the Middle Ages, Renaissance and Reformation. War is the inheritance of northern Europe. We Americans have experienced it only as liberators, not as the brutal, daily experience of occupation by the enemy.

That occupation was an agony we cannot possibly imagine: daughters of fourteen and fifteen raped in the bedrooms of their parents' homes, mother and father forced to listen to those grunts of lust; Jews taken to concentration camps;

*young men conscripted for labor in all parts of
Europe. A moral chaos best described by Jean
Moulin, leader of the French Resistance (killed
in 1943), in* Premier Combat, *the most important narrative of collapse and regeneration in
war I know.*

*Resistance to the Germans by the French my
age in the 1940s meant torture, death, a story not
yet sufficiently told. Each town I drive through
has its plaque to those civil dead, each town its
markers at odd street corners, dedicated to those
killed on August 23rd, 24th, 25th, those who
"died in the Liberation of France."*

*I begin to understand why that woman's
head was shaved, "la femme scalpée." Think of
what she meant to the other French people in
that village, those who had lost husbands, sons,
brothers, lovers to the Germans; think of their
rage as they watched her walk through the
town square on the arm of her Nazi soldier.*

*These are the years of the French of my
generation. I feel far closer to them than I do to
my American peers. The woman I talked to
who hid an American pilot; the mayor of a
small town who kept a station on the under-
ground railroad for escaping pilots; women
who lost husbands, fathers, sons. These were
the people I helped free; these the people my
nation helped free.*

*Everywhere I go and say in my terrible
French: "J'été ici à la guerre. J'été blessé à la
Canal des Mines," everywhere, I am treated as
a hero: the maid in the hotel in Verdun refuses
to let me carry my bag, a woman smiles, a man
tips his hat, says, "Merci," and means it.*

*Does my wound at last begin to make sense?
My journey to France and my place of*

combat joins the boy of nineteen and the man of fifty-nine, links them in that terrible understanding of the pride, pain and betrayal of the wars of my century. The pride: pride that I was there and did not run, pride that we defeated the Nazis and their holocaust. The pain, sixty million dead, three times that many wounded, cities and nations obliterated. The betrayal in the Cold War and its escalation to the threat of atomic annihilation, betrayal that always follows victory.

Bar, Left Bank
September 13, 1984

Here in Paris I watch these marvelous women, so easy with their sexuality, their style in dressing, their quick gestures, their intimacy with their flesh, femininity not repressed but an expression of their delight in life. Oh, their quick-sliding, side-flashing glances. As I watch them, I remember the voices of my mothers once again, those southern women murmuring whispers soft in saffron dusk, stars purple in night-sky. As I watch these women, I realize how much I have lost over these many many years, the loves I might have known, the pleasures of the flesh I might have enjoyed, for in my deepest self I know I always have been blocked, shut out, closed from the most intimate caress. In the deepest heart the emasculation of the wound. My double wound.

Yet, perhaps, now that I have touched that boy of nineteen again on the banks of the canal where I was wounded my son, my father, *know his fear, his courage, his strength, per-*

haps now that I am merged with him again, I can rediscover what it is to be a youth, to laugh with delight at the joy of my sex?

When I renounced my father's rifle and moved to Cape Cod, I rediscovered tenderness lost for so many years, the tenderness of my parents so long denied.

Now the boy of nineteen, the man of fifty-nine whole again, my journey through the land of the wounded is at last complete, and I have left my loneliness behind me, free to explore for the first time in my life a full relationship with a woman, the double wound to my flesh—and from my mother, her love for me, mine for her—healed.

I can accept all Mother gave me as child and youth, her marvelous caring and protection, those wonderful voices: I can incorporate her femininity into my being, accept my sensitivity and my grace as part of my humanity, no longer threatened by them, woman's flesh the greatest beauty I shall ever know, able to create that miracle denied to men, another being.

I weep real tears for so many lost decades of my struggle, so many people hurt.

The boy and the man become one at last, no longer split by the wound.

A new life now begins.

Chartres
September 18, 1984

I've come to Chartres from Paris.

I've settled in this town with the most beautiful building I have ever seen—far exceeding even those other cathedrals of my past—to meditate, read, work on the book, perhaps complete the first draft before returning to the United States.

I write every morning, come to the cathedral to meditate in the afternoon. These vast-arched open spaces rise toward my sense of God almost as if the ceiling is heaven and the stained-glass windows the sun and moon and stars sending shafts of blue and green and gold and blue and red shimmering in the air of the cathedral like newborn planets dancing in the misty light.

The miracle is that I have come here to Chartres, the church of sculpture and flying buttresses, stained glass and light, a mystical cavern, a place dedicated to the Mother, Mary, her compassion and her caring at the heart of this cathedral, the compassion and the voices of my many mothers expressed in this great building, the compassion I now take unto myself.

My life has stretched from the liberation of the cathedral at Reims to Chartres, its highest points Salisbury, Santiago de Compestella, Lugo and Leon. These cathedrals of the Middle Ages speak of other times, eras even more violent than our own, but times when places of compassion, devoted to the symbol of compassion, Mary, were constructed by whole societies: kings and queens and lords gave money; burghers and members of guilds donated stained-glass windows; peasants contributed their labor. The tradition of Mary was devoted to the miracle of caring in the midst of such brutality and rage that we can scarcely imagine it, cathedrals the only places free of killing grounds.

Mary stood, far more than Christ, for a tradition of peace and love: she nurtured men in their pain. This, the same gift of wisdom my mothers gave to me—born of a similar brutality, killing grounds of the Civil War, born of men wounded and killed in that war, women who made places for their children free of killing grounds—just as Mary's cathedrals offered sanctuary to the children of an entire culture.

In my journey through the land of the wounded in this century of war, I have learned that compassion is all that survives. Compassion, which accepts the violence upon earth, violence so deep in men and nature; compassion, which is able to exist within violence and not be destroyed by the violence about it, an island of security in a frightening world; compassion, which is neither masculine nor feminine but rises above sex and gender; compassion, which embraces the enemy outside of killing grounds and our rifles; compassion, which always demands social justice. Compassion, God's gift to humanity.

Settled deep into this understanding at last, the man of fifty-nine reunited with the boy of nineteen, both linked to art, nature, God, our children, living by the voices of our many mothers, no longer the rifles of our fathers, roots reaching back and back and back into deepest time here in this cathedral, I rise and leave, returning to my home, my journey through the land of the wounded at last complete, a journey taken in solitary honor.

DEBTS OF THANKS

There are so many institutions and people who have helped me over my lifetime; I list them below. I would particularly like to remember:

The United States Army Medical Corps and the Veterans Administration, the first for saving my life, the second for assistance in preserving it;

Mallary and Christine Fitzpatrick, who stand, in my mind, for the best people can become;

John Gilchrist, Jack Hall and John Wax. Beginning forty-five years ago, their loving support has been an essential root of my life, helping me master the pain and confusion of my wound;

Martha Gordan, who helped in a period of great travail;

The Huckabees;

John and Noa Williams, who have supported my work over time;

Siena Sanderson, for her careful and critical reading of this and all my manuscripts;

Richard McDonough, my agent, whose support has given me such impetus at moments of despair;

Henry A. Sauerwein, Jr., whose conversation and intellect always stimulate me;

The Wurlitzer Foundation, which Henry directs, for its grants;

Alan Wells, Charlie Johnson, Pat D'Andrea and Janet Byrne, who read early drafts and gave me great encouragement;

Pat Frederick, my editor, who picked my manuscript from the pile and whose sharp ear, clear mind and firm determination have made this into a much better book;

Paul Fussell, who read this book in galleys and gave support;

Ted Dow as well;

And, always, Elaine . . .

* * *

In addition, my thanks to those who have given me their friendship and caring over time: Paul Berger, John Day, William C. Montgomery, Jr., Donald Mulligan, Robert E. Reed, John Culp, Sidney and Cynthia Brower, Norman and Mickey Klein, Harry Broley, Sarajane Johnson, Gordon Brigham, Natasha Shylnik, Lisa Peattie, Tunney Lee, Lilian Kemp, Imadiel Ariel, Diane Tabor, Richard Boraggio, Shirley Fuller, Ruth Hayden, Bob and Margaret Pyle, Elizabeth Maiden, Bob and Madeleine Watt, Lillian Corey, Steve and Lucy Allen, David Van Meter, Robert Baron and *all* of Fulcrum's great staff.